The Biblical Meaning of History

BY SIEGFRIED J. SCHWANTES

Pacific Press Publishing Association
Mountain View, California

Omaha, Nebraska

Calgary, Alberta

Contents

To the loving memory of my parents

Library of Congress Catalog Card No. 70-99960

Introduction

Meaninglessness is intolerable to intelligent human beings. Man's most noble efforts urge him to make sense out of the universe and to define his role in it. The quest for significance drives him onward. For centuries man has searched and toiled, naïvely assuming that if the riddles of nature were solved, then the riddle of restless man—feet planted on the earth, thoughts soaring to the stars beyond—would be solved as well. Pinning his hopes on newly found tools of scientific research, he aspires someday to reduce the problems of the physical universe to one elegant, all-inclusive equation.

Simultaneously with the attack on the broad front of physical research another less spectacular quest has been going on in historical research. G. B. Vico, with considerable insight, remarked in his *Scienza nuova* that since God created nature, He alone holds the key to its mysteries; but since history is man's own creation, man is well qualified to probe into its secrets. Written early in the eighteenth century, his book remained forgotten for several generations. But as congenial minds became increasingly aware that history rather than science might hold the clue to the enigma of human destiny, successive scholars refined the tools of scientific historical inquiry, and advances were made into all periods under scrutiny. The ground was divided among an enlarging army of specialists, and, as might be expected, data were amassed in bewildering profusion. Archaeological discoveries brought to light unknown cultures and civilizations. Dead languages were deciphered. Hieroglyphic and cuneiform inscriptions yielded the secrets of Egypt and Mesopotamia. The frontiers of knowledge were pushed back in every direction, and scholars had for the first time four millennia of documented history before their eyes. The past truly came alive.

Nevertheless, this mountain of data brought man no nearer to that which lay closest to his heart, namely, the meaning of history. Where is history leading after all? Some philosophers reflecting over the broad canvas of man's past thought they could discern some pattern, some recognizable trend. Others with equal emphasis denied the evidence for any intelligible design. The historicists argued convincingly that man steeped in the historical continuum could not pass judgment on history *in toto*. Man, no mere spectator, but enmeshed in history as actor, could not speak objectively about meaning in history. Man needed what the positivist historian denied him, an Archimedean point outside of history to appraise the past with detachment.

Yet this is exactly what the Christian revelation provides, a vantage point above and beyond history, a seat in the balcony, from which the historical drama may be surveyed and recognized as a meaningful part of the divine scheme of things. "By faith we understand," says the author of the letter to the Hebrews. By faith man is "given" a divine standpoint from which to interpret reality.

Unaided reason has proven itself unable to detect meaning in history. Philosophies of history, over and again, are ceaselessly discarded as unsatisfactory. To the Greeks history repeated itself in unending cycles. The rationalists of the eighteenth century hit upon the idea of inevitable progress, an idea which grew in popularity throughout the next century when science and technology held the promise of a golden age just around the corner. But the idea of inevitable progress lost much of its credibility after the insanity of two world wars. The idea that the world was getting better and better was no longer a foregone conclusion. Other philosophers of history, such as Oswald Spengler, conceived human societies like biological organisms subject to the law of birth, growth, decay, and death. Writing soon after the tragedy of the first world war, Spengler was pessimistic in regard to Western civilization. To him it showed undeniable signs of decay. Spengler had much to say and was undoubtedly correct in his diagnosis of Western civilization, but he had almost nothing to say about the goal of history and offered little but despair.

To accept the providential view of history does not necessarily enable one to give a plausible explanation for every major turn of events in terms of an overruling moral providence. Any such claim would be highly presumptuous. Pertinent information is not available in most cases. Actual witnesses were seldom aware of religious implications. "Man looks on the outward appearance, but the Lord looks on the heart."[1] Proximity to an event does not always give to the observer an advantage over all others who study it.

It is axiomatic that no historian can enjoy the advantages of both

1. 1 Samuel 16:7.

proximity and perspective. History is an explanation not of current events but of *faits accomplis*. Explanations given by eyewitnesses of an event seldom satisfy those who watch from a distance. A sense of perspective is a necessary requisite for the historian for the simple reason that an event is understandable only in the context of what preceded and what followed. This means that the more that is known on both sides of an event the better it is understood. Thus we are led to the almost paradoxical conclusion that, provided he is acquainted with the links which bind past to present, the farther a historian stands from an event the better he is able to comprehend it.

But no event is linked to the present by a single series of links, whether political, economic, or religious. Any event is susceptible to more than one explanation, each equally plausible. Such explanations would run as follows: "From the point of view of art . . . ," "From the point of view of military science . . . ," et cetera, this event may be understood thus and so, to the satisfaction of those interested in that point of view.

But since, to the Christian, religion is man's ultimate concern, events to him should be understandable from a religious standpoint. All other explanations may be valid, but only this is vital. To insist that since man is within the stream of history all events must be explained from a historic viewpoint is to ignore the fact that man is a creature not only of time but of eternity as well. Man can reflect on history by the power of time-piercing thought, and by God's grace man transcends time and history.

The Christian view of history introduces meaning where other views see only chaos. It organizes the data better than any other. It is concerned not only with the process of history but with its goal. It makes sense. It is the conviction of this author that there is no more satisfying view.

Gothic King Alaric sacks Rome in A.D. 410. The fall of the Roman Empire caused anguished onlookers to believe the whole traditional universe of meaning was collapsing. Engraving. Bettmann Archive.

Chapter 1

The Quest for Meaning

History is the record of past events. Obviously not all events. History is not concerned with events in the world of nature unless they affect or are affected by events in the world of men. Nor is history concerned with all the events in which man plays a role; it deals only with events which have significance in the overall drama.

This leads us to the next basic question: What is meant by a significant event? The significance of an event is of necessity related to the scale of observation, whether the family, the clan, the nation, or all of a civilization. This might be called the criterion of inclusiveness.

Thus, for example, an earthquake might snuff out thousands of lives and yet not be significant if it had no impact on the future of a civilization. If on the contrary the earthquake explains why the civilization came to an end, or suffered partial eclipse for a time, it immediately becomes significant for the historian. Such was the case of the earthquake which destroyed the royal residence in Knossos at the end of the II-B Minoan period. There are no written records of the event, but the material destruction detected by archaeologists helps explain a gap between this and the subsequent Minoan civilization.

A second criterion might be termed the criterion of usefulness. An event is significant for the historian if it clarifies subsequent events which in turn are significant. That which explains nothing is soon discarded as useless debris. But an event which by its nature imparts meaning to many otherwise detached fragments survives in memory because of its unifying value. Not only does it survive in oral tradition, but eventually it is written into the pages of history.

Popular opinion notwithstanding, a historian is not primarily concerned with recording past events as *res gestae,* accomplished facts. He must first evaluate before he can record. Not every event is worth recording. Not even a chronicler in a medieval monastery recorded every event that occurred in the surrounding area, or even within the walls of the monastery where he lived. He, too, for lack of time if for no other reason, must record only what was significant. In all probability his superior appointed him chronicler because he had a better-than-common acumen to distinguish between the trivial and the significant. He would not record every bit of gossip spoken at mealtime, but would choose to report the demise of an abbot, the intrigues leading to the election of his successor, or the plague ravaging the countryside. Even a second-rate chronicler has enough historical sense to forget the thousand and one trivialities which do not make history.

In the epilogue to his Gospel, John mentions that he, too, did not write down every event in the short ministry of his Master. He was conscious that pragmatic selections had to be made. He must discern the dominant motif in the life of Christ and then, from the overwhelming abundance of material, choose that which was relevant to the motif. "I suppose," he remarks, "that the world itself could not contain the books that would be written."[1]

Likewise Polybius (c. 205 - c. 125 B.C.) when he retired after an eventful life to write down the history of the world from the Second to the Third Punic Wars, selected as a motif or controlling theme that of Rome's triumphant expansion in the Mediterranean, gathering his materials so as to substantiate his conviction of Rome's destiny. As far back as records go, Polybius was the first to insist on the need of an all-inclusive view to make history meaningful. Fragmentary histories were no better than edifying chronicles. Polybius is attested by professional historians. But to carry out his purpose effectively he had both to remember and to forget, to evaluate the multitude of facts and record only those which bore significance.

It goes without saying that Polybius's interpretation of the facts was colored by his presuppositions. Nobody, not even the natural scientist, discusses any subject without conscious or unconscious assumptions. The natural scientist approaches his object with the preconceived opinions that nature is intelligible, that its regularities can be expressed in laws, that the present is the measure of the past. But because the scope of scientific investigation is usually limited, no one questions these undemonstrable assumptions.

There is no such thing as a totally objective historian. No one studies the sources without any bias whatsoever. Like everyone else, the historian is steeped in the stream of history and can no more escape the prejudices of his generation than he can escape the air he breathes. He observes the past through the glasses of current philosophical outlook. In this sense history is an ongoing dialogue between the present and the past. Every new generation must rewrite past history to make it intelligible to itself.

Gibbon's views in *The Decline and Fall of the Roman Empire* might have satisfied his contemporaries circumscribed in the same philosophical and theological milieu. But the questions a historian would ask in the second half of the twentieth century would be markedly different, and the answers he would get would necessarily differ from Gibbon's. There are not significantly more facts known about Rome today than there were in Gibbon's time. Nor is there a significantly greater degree of accuracy possible in our day than in his. Distortion of facts may still occur among historians to suit one's particular point of view. But, admittedly, this becomes less and less likely as the knowledge of basic data becomes common property. The salient facts about the past are too well known to be distorted with impunity to suit partisan views. Less-known details might be used by a writer to slant the evidence in favor of this or that theory. But such distortions do not long escape detection.

Yet a modern historian using the same data as Gibbon might arrive at a totally different conclusion. He might, for example, lay the blame for the fall of the Roman Empire not at the door of the Christian religion, but at the door of the economic deterioration of the late Roman society. The ultimate conclusion hinges on the matter of the interpretation of the facts.

Facts regarding aggregates of human beings are incomparably more complex than facts regarding aggregates of molecules. The student of nature enjoys the additional advantage of being able to abstract one aspect of nature and then focus his attention upon some minor detail of that abstraction. Galileo did so in studying the laws of falling bodies. He narrowed down his observation to the barest phenomenon, surrounded with little or no ambiguity, so that a single, univocal question would obtain a single, univocal answer.

Scientists today do so as well, which accounts in part for the prodigious advances in the physical sciences. The physicist, for example, isolates radiation of a single wavelength and makes that his object of investigation. Or he singles out particles of known mass, imparts to them a known velocity in a linear accelerator, and watches the result of their collision with other particles of known mass. In either case the answers can be unambiguous because the phenomena are unambiguous.

No such advantages attend the historian. Human actions of historical significance affecting thousands or millions of people are never that simple. Compound the impossibility of subjecting past actors of the human drama to detailed analysis in depth, and it soon becomes evident why past events are interpreted differently by different historians. For instance, on the morning of the assassination of Julius Caesar what did the Roman senators individually think of Caesar? Had he no friends in the aristocratic chamber? Was their paralysis due to panic, indifference, or sympathy with the conspirators? Were Cassius and Brutus, in their love for the Republic, as idealistic as they pretended; or were they defending vested interests? These and a host of similar questions can never be unequivocally answered. Enough accurate information on all the issues simply does not exist. The data that survive are found in Livy, Suetonius, Dio Cassius—each of them more and more remote from the actual events, all of them recognizing in the murder of Caesar a capital event of Roman history, but each one sifting the available facts through the mesh of his own particular presuppositions. The questions raised by each reflected his individual political and philosophical sympathies.

A brute historical event is never as simple as a brute natural event. Worse yet, it may not, as a natural event may, be reenacted for a closer look. By its very nature the historical event is unique and unrepeatable.

This peculiarity justifies the statement that whereas science is concerned with the general, history is concerned with the particular and unique. Lincoln's assassination does not cast much light on the murder of Caesar, except perhaps by revealing common motives behind human actions. But since the actors are never the same, the motives, even though similar, are never the same either. Moreover the many subtleties in human nature preclude the assumption that identical circumstances (if such were possible) would elicit identical responses.

All of this drives us back to the admission that history is never merely a compilation of facts regarding human actions. At best this would be a chronicle dry as dust. To deserve consideration, history must of necessity involve facts *and* interpretation. Man is not satisfied merely to know that something happened even if he knew how it happened. As a rule his chief interest is to know *why* it happened, and what attendant circumstances made it likely or inevitable. As Professor M. Oakeshott once remarked, "To ask for pure narrative is to ask for pure nonsense."

As interpreter the historian's task is at least in part defined for him. According to "the principle of noetic value," only significant events normally survive in the memory of mankind. As a result only a small fraction of events which transpired in the human scene are remembered and recorded. It is the task of the historian to rediscover, if it is not obvious, the reason the surviving events were considered significant.

By the same token the task of the contemporary historian is in a sense harder, since he does not benefit from the process of noetic selection accompanying the passage of time. Imagine Callisthenes, nephew of Aristotle, attached to Alexander the Great's expedition as official historian. What would he record, and what would he leave out? One decision was just as important as another. Not every happening in camp life was worth recording, not even what occurred every day in Alexander's life. Not everything was significant from the point of view of Callisthenes qua historian. Reflections such as these led him to lose his modesty and, so it is reported, to remark in the conqueror's presence that Alexander's fame depended not on what Alexander did but on what Callisthenes wrote.

In a certain sense Callisthenes was making history as much as Alexander. "History is what historians make" remains a popular dictum among members of the profession. If in their estimation certain politicians, or certain generals, or certain gala events are not worth mentioning in their histories, such politicians, generals, and events will most likely sink into the limbo of historical oblivion.

Rather than affirm that historians make history, however, it is perhaps truer to say that history is a view of the past through the eyes of a historian. No historian would omit the name of Alexander from the record. Independent of contemporary written records, Alexander made enough of an impact on the world of his day to be remembered otherwise. A dozen cities were erected to perpetuate his memory. After his adventurous career, life in the Near East was never the same. An account of him would have been given, if not by Callisthenes, then by someone else. Someone would explain why the course of events veered so dramatically in the centuries following Alexander.

Some events are so outstanding they simply cannot be ignored. No historian, for example, studying France in the eighth and subsequent centuries, could ignore Charlemagne. His presence in documents and monuments rears as imposing as the Alps in Switzerland. But without Alcuin, Charlemagne's provost in matters of education, who wrote the history of education in medieval France, the history of education would show a yawning gap.

On the other hand, the teachers Alcuin assigned to different schools are barely known, if at all. Their names, we must conclude, have almost no historical significance. They lived their little lives, but if one or another had never lived, history would still be much the same.

To be significant, events must cause more than a passing ripple on the surface of national life. They must be depth charges felt by future generations. There is no such thing as the "democracy of events," as Karl Popper would have us believe. To affirm that all events are equally significant is to deny that the memory of mankind is itself selective. Erich Kahler in his provocative book, *The Meaning of History,* makes this point emphatic. "Rome, I dare say, was more important than Phrygia, Augustine more important than Donatus of Carthage, Luther more important than Karlstadt. There are shifts of prominence from one country to another, from one kind of human activity and interest to another."[2]

The judgment of the significance of events is also bound with the field of interest the investigator has under study, as suggested above. To the historian of music the seventeenth-century Italian composer Palestrina is of great interest. Palestrina is a significant link in the evolution of musical composition. His fine counterpoint helps explain the musical accomplishments of J. S. Bach and his spiritual heirs. But his name might with good reason be ignored by a political historian. In the political arena his career played no significant role.

This consideration brings up this crucial question: Which human activity exerts the preponderant influence in history. Art? Politics? Economics? Religion? No one answer would enlist universal support.

Is history to be taken as "the story of liberty," as Benedetto Croce evaluated it? Or as the story of social justice, or equal economic opportunities for all? Most history books are heavily slanted toward the political aspect of history. Statesmen and generals claim the lion's share in most studies of the past. While purporting to describe the march of civilization, historians assume that the struggle for political dominance best characterizes man's life on earth. The scholar who assumes that wars of expansion best describe a given civilization will choose from the storehouse of ascertainable facts those which seem to support his thesis and will interpret them according to his political philosophy. By choosing some facts, dismissing others, and organizing his material so that later facts seem to evolve naturally from earlier, he arrives at a relatively consistent view of the past. Another historian, working under the same assumptions, might present a more consistent exposition either by incorporating more facts of significance, or by interpreting the same facts in a more convincing way.

Facts rarely speak for themselves. An array of well-attested facts does not *ipso facto* make history. Nor will it suffice to say that "facts are sacred and interpretation is free." Facts by themselves are dead parts until a historian organizes them into a meaningful whole. They acquire meaning as parts of an intelligible whole. Touched with the magic wand of meaning, facts come alive.

Events become meaningful in colligation with other events. Out of context an event conveys no more meaning than a chord apart from its score. Wilberforce's campaign for the abolition of the slave trade early in the nineteenth century makes sense in conjunction with contemporary events, in England and elsewhere, in the contest for the recognition of human dignity which followed in the wake of the French Revolution. The Seven Years' War which tore Europe in the days of Frederick the Great of Prussia is only understood as an episode of a longer drama. Cast against the background of European politics which hinged on the concept of the balance of power, its inception and denouement become intelligible.

There is an inner logic in the sequence of events which, when revealed by the historian, obtains the assent of like minds. This inner logic is bound with the commonsense expectation that under given circumstances individuals or groups behave according to some familiar pattern. Human nature, being what it is, inclines the historian to anticipate one possible response rather than another.

This is not to say that there is an intrinsic inevitability in the sequence of events. If there were no alternative to any given situation, one might speak of laws of history, and political events might become as predictable as natural events. This belief is still entertained by die-hard determinists. But human reactions to the same set of circumstances vary within a broad range. At most we may speak of probabilities. In most historical explanations our minds are satisfied if the sequence of events falls within a reasonable spectrum of expected alternatives. If it does not, we are justified in calling the explanation into question. In such cases, more often than not, one or more significant facts remain ignored. With the additional information taken into account, the reconstructed sequence of events appeals to our intelligence, and we are satisfied by the explanation.

The meaning of a part is found only in the wider context of the whole. To the biologist the cell acquires meaning in terms of the tissue, the tissue in terms of the organ, and the organ in terms of the organism. Likewise to the historian an event acquires meaning in terms of a chain of events or epoch, the epoch in terms of a civilization, and the civilization in terms of universal history. Man's quest for meaning in history may, according to the depth of his inquiry, stop at any level of partial understanding. For practical purposes man's inquisitiveness is often satisfied when the object of his question is explained by the next higher level of comprehensiveness.

Though partial understanding may satisfy practical needs, yet restless man is bound to pursue the quest for ultimate meaning. No half-hearted affirmations will satisfy him. Some innate drive urges him on. Just as the meaning of physical nature must be sought beyond nature in metaphysics, the ultimate meaning of history must be sought beyond history. Man needs and demands a higher point of view.

Those who refuse to transcend the historical plane must by this very fact conclude that there is no meaning to universal history. They reach an impasse. But, whereas unaided reason sees nothing but unfathomable mystery, Biblical faith sees God as the Lord of history. To faith, history acquires meaning in the broader context of an eternal order—God's order. Human history with its light and shadow, its achievements and defeats, hopes and frustrations, is viewed by Biblical man *sub specie aeternitatis* as part of a wider reality. Of course this wider reality can only be apprehended by faith. "Through faith we understand," wrote the author of Hebrews.[3] "Behind the dim unknown" faith sees God, who, as the Lord of all life, imparts meaning both to individual existence and to the somber expanse of universal history.

As remarked above, the concept of meaning is indissolubly bound with the concept of order, a divine order. This divine order is to be understood not as static, but as dynamic and moving toward a goal of God's own choosing according to plan. Believers assume the possibility of tracing this divine plan on the pages of history. It would be idle to speak of such a plan if it must remain forever unidentifiable in the play and counterplay of events which make up human history. But admittedly the task of tracing such a plan in the maelstrom of history is comparable to the difficulty of discerning some meaningful pattern in the everchanging canvas of the clouds.

A major hurdle is that the historical records available were not written, as a rule, from the point of view of faith. They rather reflect man's pride and self-sufficiency. As a result, the believer faces an almost insurmountable task when he attempts to trace the evidences of a divine plan among the data gathered by secular spectators of the human scene. Events of religious significance were ignored in favor of others which better suited the presuppositions of the writers. What seemed of major significance politically or militarily—and that makes the bulk of recorded history—may have had only an incidental bearing on the religious drama. It is a truism that each historian chose, recorded, and stressed those events which supported his view of reality. Historians more often than not concern themselves with what happened on the battlefield, and little about the "great searchings of heart"[4] which accompany every major turn in history. But it is precisely these "searchings of heart," the great moral and spiritual decisions, which would illumine the outworking of a divine plan in history. The inadequacy of a secular exposition of man's past is not due to malicious intent, but to the historian's inability to probe beneath the surface. It is as though an observer should describe the ocean off the coast of Newfoundland in the spring by counting the icebergs floating on the great blue expanse, while ignoring that nine tenths of the bulk of those icebergs lies beneath the surface, and that mighty currents orient those mountains of ice according to a definite pattern. Professional training notwithstanding, the truth remains that the secular chronicler is more readily impressed by events which shake the political scene, while remaining blind to movements of religious significance, because the latter are "spiritually discerned."[5] And since the Christian historian, in spite of the best intentions, is likewise limited in his ability to probe beneath the surface of events and get an insight into the undercurrents of spiritual tensions and hopes, a fully convincing account of history as moving toward a divine goal may forever remain beyond his reach. Faith alone is able to bridge the gap between objective data and ultimate meaning.

As a man of faith, the Christian historian has no apology to offer for his conviction that history conforms to a divine pattern. This persuasion is but a corollary of a still higher conviction; namely, that God *is* and that He *is in control*. He is not so sanguine as to claim the ability to discern the divine purpose in any given event or series of events. But neither is he prepared to surrender his belief that history viewed as a whole bears witness to God's involvement.

The task of reinterpreting history in a way consistent with the Christian faith poses a perennial challenge to the Christian historian. That previous attempts no longer satisfy us is no reason to give up the enterprise as fruitless. Augustine was not satisfied with Eusebius's theodicy, so he composed *The City of God*. He took up a task nobly conceived in Eusebius's *Praeparatio evangelica* and carried it much farther as the light of his superior genius directed him. Three generations had gone by; new issues pressed for explanation. Rome had been sacked by Alaric at the head of the Visigoths in A.D. 410, and to anguished onlookers it seemed as if the traditional universe of meaning were collapsing. But no great idea is erected upon a vacuum. The preliminary spadework of Eusebius and Sextus Africanus was essential to the grand conception of the bishop of Hippo. To use the trite dictum ascribed to Newton, Augustine saw farther because he was standing on the shoulders of giants. Augustine found no worthy successor in the dreary centuries that followed. Neither Gregory of Tours, nor Isidore of Seville, nor the Venerable Bede felt the urge to compose a new theodicy. They contented themselves with writing histories of limited scope. Their chief handicap was that they allowed the turmoil of the barbaric invasions to cramp their perspective. They did not even try to fit events of their time into a divine scheme—even a crudely conceived scheme of their own making. Augustine, on the other hand, though a contemporary of the Visigothic sweep through Italy, was sufficiently removed from the scene of action in the safety of his bishopric on the opposite side of the Mediterranean, to be able to reflect on the vaster implications of the breakdown of the empire. In the estimation of the Middle Ages Augustine had satisfied the quest for meaning in history so well that nothing more remained to be said.

The Protestant Reformation produced no outstanding philosophy of history. Reformers were too busy changing the ecclesiastical establishment to engage in historical reflections. The barren evangelical scholasticism that followed, coupled with the religious wars that kept Europe in turmoil for another century, proved equally unproductive. Not until Bossuet in the late seventeenth century was the problem of meaning in history again taken up. Bossuet, the most eloquent Catholic prelate of his time, tutor of the French dauphin, stood squarely on the providential view of history, which rightly came to be identified with the Biblical view. A generation later Voltaire and the rationalists of the Enlightenment took issue with Bossuet's view. In French rationalistic circles, and subsequently elsewhere, the providential understanding of history was discarded as naïve and replaced by the view of inevitable progress. Supposedly backed by the scientific outlook in vogue, it remained under one guise or another the prevailing view till our days. Two world wars of catastrophic consequences undermined the optimistic dogma of inevitable progress. The comfortable moorings reason had built proved unreliable, and man was adrift once more in the quest for meaning in history. Of man's predicament under the existential threat of meaninglessness, the countless books on the interpretation of history published during the last quarter of a century give eloquent witness.[6]

This volume is written under the conviction that the Biblical view of history retains its validity and deserves candid consideration. Many of the so-called "scientific reasons" for rejecting it, which sounded plausible one or two generations ago, are no longer tenable. Nor is there cause for allowing the many nihilistic existentialist views undisputed ground. The following two chapters, "Chance and Providence" and "Providence and Freedom," aim at answering the more serious objections to the Biblical view. They should serve as an introduction to a systematic exposition of the Biblical meaning of history in the remainder of the book.

NOTES AND REFERENCES

1. John 21:25.
2. Erich Kahler, *The Meaning of History,* page 193.
3. Hebrews 11:3.
4. Judges 5:15, RSV.
5. 1 Corinthians 2:14.
6. See for example, N. Berdyaev, *The Meaning of History* (1936); Paul Tillich, *The Interpretation of History* (1936); John Macmurray, *The Clue to History* (1939); C. R. North, *The Old Testament Interpretation of History* (1946); E. C. Rust, *The Christian Understanding of History* (1947); Reinhold Niebuhr, *Faith and History* (1949); Karl Löwith, *Meaning in History* (1949); Herbert Butterfield, *Christianity and History* (1949); John Baillie, *The Belief in Progress* (1951); Eric Voegelin, *Order and History* (1956); M. C. D'Arcy, *The Meaning and Matter of History* (1961); J. M. Connolly, *Human History and the Word of God* (1965).

Chapter 2

Chance and Providence

God through His providence is active in both nature and history. This providential view was a basic presupposition of the Biblical writers and was tacitly assumed by Christian thinkers through the Middle Ages and beyond. Yet it was not until the end of the seventeenth century that it found its classical expression in the book *Discours sur l'histoire universelle* by the French bishop J. B. Bossuet.

Scarcely had the ink dried on Bossuet's manuscript, however, when the view was challenged by Voltaire in his *Essai sur les moeurs*. Reflecting the temper of the Age of Enlightenment, Voltaire opposed reason to revelation and natural progress to providence. With vitriolic ink he exposed Bossuet as an obscurantist whose knowledge of history was pitifully inadequate and whose religious faith blinded him to a naturalistic explanation of the facts. To many, Voltaire's attack on the providential view of history remained the last word on the subject. Many yet share his viewpoint, despite the fact that the classical physics of the eighteenth and nineteenth centuries on which his arguments hinged has largely been superseded by the concepts of quantum physics and its varied implications.

Belief in God's providential activity is part of the warp and woof of Biblical faith. The author of Hebrews makes this faith explicit by stating, "He [Christ] reflects the glory of God and bears the very stamp of His nature, upholding the universe by His word of power."[1] The same dynamic word that called the physical universe out of nothing upholds it in harmonious coherence. Scripture never pictures the universe as a self-operative machine running in perpetual independence of its Creator.

Certainly it operates with a predictable regularity. Scientists have gradually uncovered the operation of such regularities in ever-wider fields and have expressed their understanding of them in the so-called laws of nature.

But the existence of laws of nature does not exclude the need of a sustaining providence any more than the civil laws of the land exclude the need of law-enforcing agents. Laws are never self-operative. They are never the cause of phenomena. They are merely man's way of describing regular behavior in nature. As man's understanding of the physical universe progresses, he expresses the regularities he observes in ever more accurate terms. Science is man's systematic attempt to discover and formulate these laws and to detect the general principles behind them.

Scientists work on the assumption that nature is basically simple and that it should be possible to arrive at some fundamental equation from which all laws might be derived mathematically. Einstein's quest for a unified field equation that would explain all optical, electrical, and gravitational phenomena was just such an attempt. But even if such an attempt should succeed, still the basic fact remains that laws only tell us *how* nature operates, never *why*. Laws describe phenomena, never originate them. The need of a Prime Mover, a Creator and Sustainer of the universe, remains untouched. Jesus stated this truth in the words, "My Father is working still, and I am working."[2]

A common fallacy is the belief that as science proceeds in its relentless march through the universe God must of necessity recede. Some assume that as more and more areas are flooded with the light of scientific research there is less and less room for divine activity. This popular misconception presupposes that God moves only in the realm of the mysterious, the dark, and the unknown. If law and order are recognized in the field of astronomy, then, some suppose, God has nothing to do with stars and galaxies. If biological laws are brought to light, then, so goes the argument, God is in no way involved in the processes of life.

Such fallacy may be understood as a reaction against the naïve explanation of natural phenomena current in the prescientific era. When the earth was thought to be populated with nymphs and gnomes, man was more prone to be amazed with the extraordinary

Voltaire speaks to Frederick II (at head of table). Voltaire attacked the ideas of Bishop Bossuet, who held that God is active in both nature and history. (See page 19.) Engraving from a work by Adolf Menzel. Historical Pictures Service, Chicago.

and the bizarre than with uniformity and orderliness. In the popular mind, eclipses and earthquakes were the more obvious manifestations of divine power. As eclipses were eventually explained and predicted, they were removed from the realm of the mysterious. To some this meant that since celestial phenomena occur according to known laws they occur independently of the will of God.

In effect the recognition that nature is orderly, that its behavior may be understood and expressed mathematically, elicited different responses from different minds. In face of the rapid progress of astronomy after the Copernican discovery (of a heliocentric, or sun-centered, planetary system of which the earth was a minor component), the reactions of equally capable thinkers contrasted sharply. To some the discovery of law and predictability in the celestial movements led to a deeper admiration of God's handiwork.

One such person was German astronomer Johannes Kepler, who, on the basis of the astronomical observations collected by Tycho Brahe, discovered the three laws of planetary motion. Kepler described his epoch-making research as "thinking God's thoughts after Him." The very existence of natural laws discoverable by human intelligence was to him convincing evidence that only a divine mind could have projected the starry heavens revolving with unerring precision. To Kepler the absence of law would betray the absence of a Planner.

Another such person was the English mathematician Sir Isaac Newton, who ranked among the leading physicists of his day. With characteristic candor Newton recognized his indebtedness to previous generations of thinkers. But above all he saw no conflict between his thinking as a scientist and his belief in God and providence. Besides his pioneering work in calculus and in the discovery of the laws of inertia, of gravitation, of the refraction and dispersion of light, he found time to apply himself to the study of the Scriptures, even to write a commentary on Daniel.

On the other hand the progressive discovery of the orderliness of the physical universe led not a few thinkers to the conclusion that God was an absentee landlord, who having created the universe left it to run according to secondary laws. Such were the deists of the seventeenth century and their philosophical heirs. As a rule, they did not deny the existence of God; but they did deny in various degrees

God's involvement in the regular order of nature. That is to say, they denied providence, God's personal concern for what goes on in the universe. Divine intervention in answer to prayer was regarded as tantamount to miracle, and miracles in their strictly deterministic concept of nature were taboo.

The dilemma thus posed to the Christian believer was obvious. Providence implies God's freedom to act through and above the laws of His creation. But in a universe inexorably governed by natural law, every event was conceived as already predetermined, ruling out any such activity. Laplace, the author of *Mécanique céleste,* went so far as to say that if the masses and velocities of all particles composing the universe were known, then all future events would be mathematically predictable. According to such a view, the whole future is already contained in, and absolutely determined by, the past. Milič Čapek describes the view concisely: "In the classical deterministic scheme novelty and becoming were virtually eliminated. The future was regarded as implicitly contained in the present."[3] In such intellectual climate, religious faith was bound to suffer.

Philosophical arguments notwithstanding, those who believed in providence could not surrender this basic Christian assumption. With or without the comfort of the prevailing scientific view, these Christian believers knew in their inmost hearts that God heard their prayers. In the secret recesses of their consciences, God confronted them. In this realm, beyond all the probing of science, they were aware of their own freedom and responsibility. In the inner sanctum of their souls they knew what it meant to worship God "in spirit and truth," and there caught glimpses of what Paul meant when he said, "The Lord is the Spirit, and where the Spirit of the Lord is, there is freedom.[4]

Historically the Christian does not renounce his faith because the metaphysics of the day is unfavorable. Aware that more than once the prevailing philosophical climate has changed in the blowing intellectual wind, his insights go deeper and truer than the insights of unaided reason. He can afford to wait patiently for ultimate vindication. "He who believes will not be in haste."[5]

How this vindication may take shape is illustrated in a recent book by William G. Pollard, *Chance and Providence*. This book, published in 1958, deals, as its subtitle indicates, with "God's action in a world governed by scientific law." Its author is a prominent scientist, director of the Oak Ridge Institute of Nuclear Studies. Pollard shows how advances in theoretical physics in the last few decades have shattered the concept of rigid determinism. Discoveries in atomic physics replaced laws expressing strict causation in nature with laws of statistical probability.

Pollard says, "The typical situation in science is one in which several alternatives are open in each natural process."[6] This means that there are many alternative ways in which an atom, for example, may respond when acted upon by another atomic particle. Laws will express degrees of probability favoring one alternative among many. Gone from the realm of atomic phenomena is the fixity of the cause-and-effect relationship. As statistical tables of insurance companies predict with accuracy how many people of an age-group will die in a given year, but can affirm nothing concerning the death of any individual, so natural laws predict the behavior of a great number of atoms under defined experimental conditions, but can affirm nothing concerning the individual atom.

Lurking uneasily in some minds is the thought that, given more time, science may overcome this element of indeterminacy which upset the neat scheme of physical causation ever since Heisenberg enunciated the "uncertainty principle" in 1927. But, as Pollard makes clear, the trend of scientific investigation has been toward confirming rather than undermining this concept of indeterminacy in the scale of atomic phenomena. The indeterminacy is not introduced by man in the course of experiment because of faulty apparatus, but it is objective in the sense that it is embedded in nature. It is there, whether observed by man or not. All evidence accumulated during the last forty years points to the conclusion that the concept of indeterminacy is not a transient fad among physicists, but it is here to stay. "Whether we like it or not," says Dr. Pollard, "it seems to be a world in which indeterminacy, alternative, and chance are real aspects of the fundamental nature of things, and not merely the consequence of our inadequate and provisional understanding."[7]

Nor is the objection valid that the principle of indeterminacy operates only in the atomic scale and is not applicable to large-scale phenomena like that of Newton's falling apple. The only difference is that statistically the behavior of a large number of molecules is more narrowly predictable than that of a small number. In extreme instances the several alternatives of a typical case are narrowed down to a single possibility. The situation is like that of insurance companies which stake their hope of profit on the life expectancy of a large number of individuals, which can be very accurately foreseen, whereas little can be affirmed concerning the individual policyholder, except, if you will, that he does not have a chance in a hundred of living beyond ninety or a chance in a thousand of becoming a centenarian.

As indeterminacy seems to be inherent in the fundamental nature of things, the older view that the future of the physical universe is absolutely conditioned by the present is no longer tenable. If this is true of nature, it should be even more true of man who transcends nature by the power of thought. The view long held of strict determinism in history must be likewise replaced by the concept of the openness of history. At every turn of events history is confronted with innumerable alternatives. Which alternative will be taken is, from the secular point of view, purely a matter of chance. But from the point of view of faith, the alternative taken may be a matter of Providence.

Science can no longer make any valid objection against this view. All it knows is that many alternatives are open at every turn. Why *this* is chosen and not *that* is beyond science's competence to say. Because it has nothing else to say, it gives to the uncertainty surrounding every turn of events the name of chance. Chance, then, let it be clearly understood, explains nothing. Chance is not a new factor brought into the house of science through the back door. It simply expresses that, in any given conjuncture, beyond the fact that several alternatives are possible, science has nothing to say.

But this new realization of the openness of history is exactly what the Christian recognizes as opportunity for divine providence. Without doing violence to man's freedom and attending physical circumstances, God may direct the course of events according to the unfathomable decisions of His holy will. As Dr. Pollard expresses it, "The Christian sees the chances and accidents of history as the very warp and woof of the fabric of providence which God is ever weaving."[8]

The incompatability of a deterministic view with the providential view of history was sensed by many Bible students, even though they were unable to articulate it in terms of the new insights first gained in quantum physics. B. J. Lonergan, aware of the new scientific climate, writes, "World process is open. It is the succession of probable realizations of possibilities. Hence, it does not run along the iron rails laid down by the determinists nor, on the other hand, is it a nonintelligible morass of merely chance events."[9] There is rhyme and reason in history, and yet the future is to be regarded as fluid and open both to man's freedom of choice and God's guidance.

Oscar Handlin in *Chance or Destiny: Turning Points in American History* (1955) elaborates the point that chance played an uncanny role in American history. In his prologue he makes this provocative remark: "Pondering the degree to which accident overturned the schemes of wise men, Prince Bismarck once commented that there was a special providence for drunkards, fools, and the United States. And indeed from the point of view of the experienced statesman or the professional soldier there was much to be said for the argument that America has survived and grown by a miraculous streak of luck that, at one turning point after another, directed fortune its way." The noncommitted historian can only speak of a "miraculous streak of luck," where the Christian believer may recognize the hand of Providence guiding events according to His own inscrutable design.

Nor is Oscar Handlin alone in his contention that chance is inextricably intertwined with the fabric of history. Collingwood in his illuminating philosophy of history observes that for Eduard Meyer "the proper object of historical thought is historical fact in its individuality, and that chance and free will are determining causes that cannot be banished from history without destroying its very essence."[10] One would scarcely agree with E. Meyer in labeling chance an effective "cause." But for sake of argument it is significant that prestigious historians frankly admit events might have turned out differently, and that if one alternative became real rather than another, then that occurrence was indeed a matter of "chance."

Events, particularly human events, can no longer be regarded as mere links in a chain of cause and effect. Trivial things as a shifting wind, a courtier's shyness, a metal's failure, or a soldier's blunder, to use examples cited by O. Handlin, made all the difference in the turn of a battle or the issue of a war. Reason sees only the shape of Cleopatra's nose, or the whims of Napoleon, or the fortuitous concurrence of natural phenomena as "the ingredients that determine the zigzags of history." But faith discerns beneath such seeming trivialities the inscrutable outworking of God's all-wise purpose.

Are we justified in transferring the insights gained in atomic physics to the realm of history? To this question one might reply: Is there any reason to believe that historical events are more strictly determined than natural events on the scale of the atom? To put the question is to answer it. Historical events which deserve to be so called are always the product of thought. To understand a historical event one must recapture the thought that, as Collingwood puts it, fleeted through the minds of the actors. Behind the actions there were thoughts, and the actions cannot be more strictly determined than the thoughts which gave them birth. According to H. Butterfield, the historian from Cambridge, "The texture of history is . . . as light as gossamer, light as the thought of a person merely thinking it, and its patterns seem to change as easily as the patterns of wind on water."[11] The old concept of history as predetermined and rigid must be abandoned for the more valid understanding of the openness of history. At every moment of its onward course history confronts many alternatives. Which one will be chosen, we may well believe, depends on a divine Providence which allows human freedom.

The scientific view ushered in by quantum physics is more favorable to the Christian belief in an overruling Providence than the view offered by classical physics. In the new outlook there is place for both men and God to influence the course of events. Christians have believed this, but until recently they were hard put to show its consistency with the prevailing scientific climate.

Historians tended to be less dogmatic than the scientists because they dealt with situations involving "alternative and latitude," whereas scientists dealt with the more precise phenomena of the physical world. Atomic research, a latecomer on the scientific scene, showed that the phenomena of the physical world can also be subject to "alternative and latitude."

W. G. Pollard, who holds the unique distinction of being both a frontline scientist and a theologian, offers this lucid summary: "The enigma of history resides in the fact that every event is at one and the same time the result of the operation of universal natural laws and the object of the exercise of the divine will. As history unfolds, the world moves forward in accordance with the inner requirements of its structure and the universal laws to which it is subjected. This structure is, however, so constituted and the laws under which it operates so framed as to open innumerable alternatives. Among the chances and accidents of these alternatives history treads its amazing course, ever responding to the mighty will of the Creator and Sustainer of history and expressing in the story which it tells the mysterious working out of His hidden purpose."[12]

REFERENCES

1. Hebrews 1:3.
2. John 5:17.
3. Milič Čapek, *The Philosophical Aspect of Contemporary Physics*, page 395.
4. John 4:23; 2 Corinthians 3:17.
5. Isaiah 28:16.
6. William G. Pollard, *Chance and Providence*, page 67.
7. *Ibid.*, pp. 54, 55.
8. *Ibid.*, p. 71.
9. B. J. Lonergan, S.J., *Insight*, pages 125, 126.
10. R. G. Collingwood, *The Idea of History*, page 178.
11. H. Butterfield, *Christianity and History*, page 110.
12. W. G. Pollard, *op. cit.*, p. 114.

Chapter 3

Providence and Freedom

When no naturalistic explanation seems adequate to interpret a particular event, a nontheistic historian may employ his own idea of chance—the "historical accident." The following quotation from a recent volume on ancient civilization serves as an example: "In many ways we are forced to the conclusion that the principate Augustus founded was a historical accident resulting from the long life of the first princeps."[1] Since the classic reasons given for the success of the principate seem unsatisfactory, this secular historian resorts to the least plausible of all explanations, *e.g.*, that of historical accident.

Considering the beneficent consequences of the reign of Augustus, the remarkable stability it introduced into the political climate, and the fact that under his rule Jesus was born into the world, it seems more reasonable to label this fruitful reign providential than accidental. Though Scripture unequivocally endorses the providential view of history, it confers on no one the charisma to label some events providential and some not. It might indeed be closer to the truth to state that divine providence is an all-pervasive and silent influence shaping the whole course of history, rather than a punctiliar and cataclysmic one. It may, of course, be both; but, whereas we may be convinced of the discreet and continuing operation of providence leading all history to its appointed goal, it would seem sheer conceit on the human level to assert a "more" providential efficacy in one event than in another.

Yet most believers seem prone to share Elijah's predilection for the spectacular as the normal modus operandi of providence, overlooking the fact that the God who operates silently in nature is the same God who gently carries out His redemptive purpose in history. Even Elijah, the showman par excellence, on Mount Horeb discovered to his astonishment that God's presence was not manifest in the devouring fire, or the mighty wind, or the dreadful earthquake, as he had been inclined to believe all along, but in the "still small voice." And this is exactly what we should expect if man's freedom of choice is safeguarded. God gently prods man along in "many and various ways," but the final decision is nevertheless man's and not God's. In the final analysis God does not force human action with overwhelming persuasive power. Yet this very gentleness of divine guidance becomes a stumbling block to believers and unbelievers alike. A generation, even a century, is often too short a span of time to judge the direction divine Providence is moving, almost but not quite justifying the skepticism of naturalistic philosophy. Only over the broad sweep of the centuries does the majestic scope of God's providential design become evident to human perception.

Eusebius, church historian, of Caesarea (c. 260 - c. 340), despite the limited knowledge at his disposal, intuited that the broken threads of mankind's past could be woven into a meaningful whole if history were seen as a *praeparatio evangelica,* preparation for the gospel. Only thus, in his thinking, could the incongruities of history with all its woes and unfulfilled hopes be interpreted as the concretion of a divine plan. Drawing his main inspiration from the writings of Paul, Eusebius recognizes in history an intelligible pattern. History to him moves toward a goal of God's own choice. This is equivalent to saying that history, as the totality of events affecting men in society, is under divine guidance. History, as Vico so plainly recognized,[2] is man's creation; but it is under God's direction.

This is not to say that history proves God. History reveals God to the eye of faith in the same manner that nature reveals God to the eye of faith. Of God's overruling providence in history there is evidence enough to sustain faith, though never so overwhelming as to compel it. Thus history makes sense to the believer, while remaining an insoluble riddle to the unbeliever.

If the only recoverable past is made up, as R. G. Collingwood says, of those bits of purposeful action which left their mark on the political, economic, aesthetic, or religious scene, it would be strange if the historical past, itself the result of thought, showed no intelligible pattern. Purposeful past actions can be understood and recovered because there is some logic to them. The historian is sure that the same logic which operated in Caesar's mind as he crossed the Rubicon is the logic which operates in his own mind today, otherwise he would be unable to understand Caesar's actions. Logical thought, then, is the only link which binds the historian with the past makers of history. Should we then conclude that certain particular fragments of the past are intelligible because they are acts of deliberate thought, but that the whole is not intelligible because there is no logic to it? Certainly not. Yet this is the position taken by historians who insist that they see no pattern in history.

But if some deny pattern in history, other students of man's past with equal emphasis affirm it. Thus Hegel, reviewing the decisive events from the Reformation to the French Revolution, detected a trend toward the enfranchisement of the common man. It would have been impossible to live in Europe in the early part of the nineteenth century and not hear the bell of liberty ringing over ever-widening territories. The concept of enlarging freedom became to Hegel, as it did to Benedetto Croce two generations later, the "explanatory principle of the course of history."[3]

Recognition of a pattern does not necessarily commit one to a deterministic view of history. It is possible to admit a general providence guiding the broad outlines of history, yet allow a broad scope for individual freedom. Just as in the atomic scale events are serially bound, not by links of rigid causality, but by links of greater or lesser probability; likewise in the stage of history human decisions do not necessarily produce a single unequivocal result, but rather one of several possible alternatives.

These possible alternatives are not haphazard or contradictory; otherwise planning would become impossible. The pages of history swarm with examples of careful plans wrecked on the shoals of what seem blind accidents. Alexander's plans for conquering Arabia were wrecked by his untimely death in Babylon. The same fate met Julius Caesar's grandiose program when he entered the senate on the Ides of March, 44 B.C., against the advice of friends. Julian the Apostate's scheme to reestablish pagan religion in the Roman Empire, Napoleon's dream to conquer Russia, and Hitler's to establish a united Europe under the aegis of the Third Reich were all carefully wrought, yet smashed by circumstances.

Plans are made because men count on a reasonable chance that they will produce the desired results. Yet it is never more than a reasonable chance, with the same expectancy as that of becoming rich on the stock market. Despite the odds to the contrary, men keep making plans because there is some logic in the results. If all plans miscarried, man would have stopped planning long ago. There would be no history to tell, because only purposeful and deliberate actions can be rethought by the historian. Nonetheless, the obstinate fact remains: Plans miscarry. The ever-present possibility of failure is therefore evidence of the openness of history.

There is then, as Isaiah Berlin remarked, no such thing as total historical inevitability. "The evidence for a thoroughgoing determinism is not to hand; and if there is a persistent tendency to believe in it in some theoretical fashion, that is surely due far more to a 'scientistic' or metaphysical ideal, or to a longing to lay down moral burdens, or minimize individual responsibility and transfer it to impersonal forces which can be safely accused of causing all our discontents, than to any increase in our powers of critical reflection or any improvement in our scientific techniques."[4]

The Biblical view of history rejects causal determinism as undermining personal responsibility, basic to Biblical understanding of man as created in God's image. It also rejects the view that history is completely undetermined, *e.g.*, that it presents no recognizable pattern. The view it does uphold is that history remains ever within God's reach. This view thus preserves man's freedom of choice and responsibility while maintaining God's overall guidance of the course of history.

Providence may use any of several alternatives to direct unfolding events according to a divine plan. This divine supervision is admittedly discreet so as not to thwart man's freedom on one hand, nor to deprive him of the necessity of walking by faith on the other. Though never obtrusive, divine providence is as pervasive as the air.

For a historian to introduce chance or accident as an explanatory principle is in fact to disclaim any knowledge of the real cause. Chance is not an efficient cause. To appeal to "historical accidents" is to admit ignorance of efficient causes. As an explanatory principle chance is the last plea of ignorance.

A. J. Toynbee refers to the experience which came to young Gaius Julius Caesar about the year 76 B.C., when he was on his way from Rome to Rhodes. By accident he fell into the hands of pirates, in whose company he spent some unpleasant days. Toynbee then remarks, "If his captors had chosen to liquidate him, as he did liquidate them after he had purchased his release, the world's history might have taken a different course."[5] Pascal proposed the famous *if* concerning Cleopatra's nose: Suppose that Cleopatra's nose had been longer. In fact, a seventeenth-century historian wrote a whole volume on what might have been the history of the world if Caesar had not been murdered.[6]

Speculation on the "if's" of history are sterile except to stress the element of contingency in history. Events turned at times on what seem to us mere trifles. If it had not rained on the morning of the battle of Waterloo, Napoleon's artillery, on which he so heavily relied, might have been maneuvered to advantage and the defeat turned into victory. In chapter 4 of Oscar Handlin's thought-provoking book on accidents which shaped American history, he expatiates on the chance encounter between Confederate General A. P. Hill's division foraging for supplies in Gettysburg and Union General John Buford's cavalry division, the advance guard of the Army of the Potomac. Drawn unexpectedly into the fray, the two armies began the four-day battle that would "determine the fate of the Confederacy and the Union."[7] Concerning the American Revolution he speaks of "the luck that permitted two separate armies and two separate fleets to converge at the right moment on Yorktown" and the unexpected storm which prevented English General Cornwallis from escaping the beleaguered town.[8] These two seemingly capricious events conspired to bring about the defeat which determined the outcome of the war.

Historical chance has been defined as the fortuitous concurrence of several causes, none of which could produce the given result, but which together bring it about. The probability that such causes would concur at one point is minimal, eliciting the explanation that by fortune or accident they did in fact concur. The Christian substitutes

Gaius Julius Caesar. On his way from Rome to Rhodes young Caesar was captured by pirates. He purchased his release and then later had his captors liquidated. Antique sculpture in Capitoline Museum, Rome. Historical Pictures Service, Chicago.

"providence" for "fortune or accident" and insists that providence makes use of or brings together the alternatives so as to draw the best result coherent with the divine plan.

Rejecting the deterministic view of history, H. H. Rowley, an outstanding Old Testament scholar, expounds his Biblical view as follows: "The history of today is born of the situation of yesterday, yet it is never wholly determined by that situation. . . . There is never anything inevitable in the course of the development, as though it is only a continual bringing into the light of what was already latent and implicit."[9]

There are, of course, historians who are committed to neither the deterministic nor the providential view of history. When confronted with unexpected denouements, as historians often are, they have no other resource than to appeal to, in the words of one, the "fortuitous concurrence of lucky factors." Yet the providential view is not inconsistent with sound scholarship. While it makes allowance for God in history, it by no means discourages a thorough investigation of all the evidence available. Nor does it fear that once an event is exhaustively explained God will be explained away in the process. On the contrary, God remains the guarantor of the intelligibility of any given historical event, for He remains the guarantor of history for all time.

The fact that "history is the story of freedom" is a valuable clue in tracing the outworkings of providence in history. How could freedom, an aspiration common to man, arise out of brute matter, which shows no characteristics of freedom? This aspiration, a corollary of human dignity, could only be derived from God as spirit, for only spirit is free. "Where the Spirit of the Lord is," says Paul, "there is freedom."[10]

Man can never realize all the potentialities of his being except in an atmosphere of freedom. Although it has not wholly effaced it, sin has distorted God's image in man. Freedom without responsibility is license, and responsibility without freedom is subservience. Man has lost his freedom in history. God's purpose, which stretches over the pages of history, was from the beginning to restore the divine image in man and thus make man again truly human and truly free.

In choosing to sin, that is, to rebel against God, man placed himself under bondage to his lower nature. Instead of living on the spiritual plane of responsibility in freedom, he fell to the carnal plane where his bondage issued in a delusion of irresponsibility, itself a form of slavery. In being responsible to no one but self, man deifies self, makes himself his god, and thus with the sin of rebellion compounds the sin of idolatry. This idolatry of the ego compels him to attempt to enslave his fellowmen, to try to force his fellow creatures to recognize his own false deity. Thus the story of history is the story of men in bondage desperately struggling for supremacy or at least freedom from this bondage.

Such is man's historical condition following his alienation from God—succinctly summarized in the Biblical sketch of the universal problem. The redemptive scheme, therefore, must include both deliverance from the bondage of self and its corollary, freedom from political bondage. "If the Son makes you free," said Jesus of Nazareth, "you will be free indeed."[11]

Political bondage degrades and dehumanizes man. But whereas deliverance from the thralldom of sin remains an individual and largely subjective experience, deliverance from political bondage looms large on the pages of history. It affects enormous masses of people. It is open for all to see. Its impact on society cannot be ignored. It is only a step in the total process of redemption, but it often is the prerequisite step for all that follows. Physical disabilities entail loss of freedom and often handicap spiritual regeneration. For this very reason the eradication of such disabilities occupied much of the earthly ministry of our Lord. Likewise political disabilities often blind men to their true dignity and make them oblivious to their supernal calling to be again children of God and thus regain their lost freedom.

Thus divine providence infuses men with an unquenchable thirst for freedom and guides the historical process in the direction of greater political freedom for the greatest number. This unquenchable thirst for freedom is the chief propelling force in history. Evidences showing this universal aspiration gradually being realized in the face of overwhelming odds, then, are to the Christian tokens that God is patiently working out His gracious design on the stage of history.

REFERENCES

1. Tom B. Jones, *Ancient Civilization,* page 399.
2. See R. G. Collingwood, *The Idea of History,* pages 63-71.
3. Benedetto Croce, *History as the Story of Liberty*, page 61.
4. Isaiah Berlin, *Historical Inevitability,* pages 75, 76.
5. A. J. Toynbee, *Hellenism,* page 188.
6. See R. G. Collingwood, *op. cit.,* p. 80.
7. Oscar Handlin, *Chance or Destiny—Turning Points in American History,* page 92.
8. *Ibid.,* p. 26.
9. H. H. Rowley, *Re-Discovery of the Old Testament,* page 25.
10. 2 Corinthians 3:17.
11. John 8:36.

Chapter 4

The Old Testament and History

Although any quest for the Biblical meaning of history would call upon the writings of the Old Testament as primary witnesses, it would be naïve to expect every book in the Sacred Canon to yield pertinent information. The writers for the most part were not philosophically oriented. The prophets, after all primarily preachers, concerned themselves more with the burning moral and religious issues of the day than with the long-range meaning of events. Nevertheless these prophets were heirs of a living religious tradition which came to include deep convictions on the great issues of history, convictions deeply colored by their understanding of God.

Undergirding the whole Old Testament is the concept of a personal God who transcends nature, a God who bound Israel to Himself in a covenant relationship by which that nation would be particularly blessed by a more intimate fellowship with the Eternal and would in turn become a blessing to all nations of the earth.[1] Central to the covenant relationship is the concept of a personal God whose people are His ultimate concern. This is not a crude first-stage anthropomorphic conceptualization of God to be, upon more mature reflection, eventually discarded. On the contrary, it remains the highest theological concept from beginning to end.

Modern concepts of God such as "the power that makes for righteousness" of Matthew Arnold or "the ground of being" of Paul Tillich are hollow, passionless, abstract formulations incapable of sustaining a living religious faith. C. R. North complains: "The most serious difficulty that confronts many readers of the Old Testament is the very strong emphasis upon Yahweh as personal. On this the Old Testament is uncompromising; it makes not the slightest attempt to remove the stumblingblock."[2] But it is precisely this uncompromising stance which sets the Old Testament apart from all contemporary religious literature and provides its unmatched appeal.

To the prophets history is first of all a record of God's mighty acts. It is *Heilsgeschichte,* the history of redemption. To them there is, strictly speaking, no secular history. The call of Abraham, the descent of Israel into Egypt, the Exodus under the leadership of Moses, and the events at Sinai which gave cohesion to the tribes and launched them into nationhood, were chapters in the history of God's self-disclosure. To Israel history becomes the chief vehicle to reveal God's sovereignty and grace.

As a result, to a higher degree than any other nation in antiquity, Israel developed a historical consciousness. History is meaningful at the outset because in its dramatic movement Israel learns to discern God's redemptive purpose. Rather than exposing a series of disconnected tableaux portraying the exploits of semi-legendary heroes, the Old Testament reveals history as a continuous outworking of a divine plan. As G. von Rad wrote: "The Old Testament writers confine themselves to representing Yahweh's relationship to Israel and the world in one aspect only, namely, as continuing divine activity in history. This implies that in principle Israel's faith is grounded in a theology of history. It regards itself as based upon historical acts, and as shaped and reshaped by factors in which it saw the hand of Yahweh at work."[3]

Unlike his contemporaries in Egypt and Mesopotamia, Biblical man demythologized nature and regarded it as the created handmaiden of God. He likewise demythologized history and looked upon it as the arena of God's activity. As G. Ernest Wright stresses, the Israelites took their eyes from nature and focused them "on the God who had revealed Himself in an extraordinary series of historical events. The knowledge of God was an inference from what actually had happened in human history. The Israelite eye was thus trained to take human events seriously, because in them was to be learned more clearly than anywhere else what God willed and what He was about."[4]

This revelatory concept of history delivered Israel from the snare of the cyclic view which bound Greek historiography, as well from the static mold of Egyptian thought with its notion of an immutable order normative for all time and precluding change. Israel was aware of change, as was Greece; but unlike Greece, Israel was aware of movement in history toward a divine goal. This awareness illumined each step in its national life and filled each crisis with meaning.

How to reconcile two basic, apparently contradictory, assumptions of Biblical history, divine sovereignty and human freedom, into a coherent scheme, poses a problem which has challenged theologians throughout the centuries. Yet it presents no hurdle to Old Testament writers. Both truths are taken for granted, and neither is allowed to diminish the force of the other. Biblical writers achieve a neat balance by never pushing either one to an absolute extreme. In the realm of history God allows latitude for man as a responsible moral agent endowed with freedom of choice. This is an underlying premise. It is a tacit assumption in the story of the Fall and in all subsequent events. Scripture never treats man as an automaton. His dignity as a person is bound with the recognition of his moral freedom. He is free to respond to God's call in love and to find therein the highest fulfillment of his freedom, or to reject that call and assume the full responsibility of his freedom to choose bondage.

Equally clear from the record is the fact that man chose to rebel against the divine order. The psalmist describes the human predicament in the words: "They have all fallen away; they are all alike depraved; there is none that does good, no, not one."[5] Much of history, as the story of man living and acting in alienation from God, bears this out. Providential forbearance allows man to build a profane order in opposition to the divine order.

But Bible writers never draw a clear-cut dichotomy between profane and redemptive history. On the one hand, man, even though in rebellion against his Creator, is nevertheless held responsible to Him. On the other hand, God never loses interest in man in spite of his recalcitrance. History, then, is never purely secular. It invariably contains an element of judgment. *Geschichte ist Gericht*—history is judgment. Not all that happens on the mundane stage happens because God wills or approves. But all that happens is allowed to happen by God and remains under His judgment. God holds man accountable for his decisions as a free moral agent. History is consequently ever freighted with moral responsibility.

To say that history is theodicy or judgment, however, is to say only half the truth. God is never portrayed in the Old Testament as a stern judge sitting aloof above a world of carnage and woe. The same Biblical writers who portray Him as present in history *through law* also portrary Him as present *in love*. God as Father is ever engaged in bringing the prodigal to *Himself,* as Francis Thomson expressed in "The Hound of Heaven":

> But with unhurrying chase
> And unperturbèd pace,
> Deliberate speed, majestic instancy,
> They beat—and a Voice beat
> More instant than the Feet—
> "All things betray thee, who betrayest Me."

This persistent pursuit of divine love after the erring son confers to all history its transcendent significance. "How can I give you up, O Ephraim! How can I hand you over, O Israel! . . . My heart recoils within Me, My compassion grows warm and tender."[6] Divine agony over rebellious man, with all its mysterious implications, makes it impossible for history to be merely profane or secular. Above the tragedies and foibles of mankind, above the din of war and struggles for power, is a divine Form, wrapped in the mists of eternity; the very thought of this Presence transmutes secular events into dimly felt intimations of a guiding Providence.

It was not mere coincidence that early in its national life Israel acquired a keen historical consciousness. This is the more remarkable when one considers that neighboring people rarely rose above the quagmire of myth. Ugarit with its temples and libraries, thriving international trade and sophisticated pageantry, the metropolis of northern Phoenicia in the fourteenth century B.C., produced no known piece of historical writing. Its literary fame is grounded solely on its crude fertility myths of Anat and Baal, Keret and Aqhat.[7] Nor is there known a single piece of historical literature from the Canaanite milieu written prior to 900 B.C. The inscription of Mesha, better known as the Moabite Stone, dating from the latter half of the ninth century B.C., is the first inscription with a clear historical intent. In length it compares with a short chapter of the book of 1 Kings. Nor are the Phoenician inscriptions of Karatepe in Cilicia, of Zenjirli in northern Syria, and elsewhere, any better than the Moabite Stone in giving evidence of a sense of historical continuity.

Israel's historical consciousness grew out of its experience of deliverance from Egyptian bondage. While in Egypt, Israel had no national history. While slaves on foreign soil, life was to them a drudgery with no particular meaning. Whatever memories still lingered from the patriarchal age were slowly eroded by hopelessness. Life without hope is devoid of meaning. And without a modicum of meaning there can be no history, only atomistic events.

Contrary to all human expectations, the deliverance foretold by Moses in the name of Yahweh came about, thus stamping a divine imprint upon the Exodus. National conscience began to awaken. Dispersive clan loyalties began to fuse into national devotion to Yahweh with a powerful moral-religious content. Israel had not been delivered merely from degrading slavery, but delivered for a transcendent purpose.

That purpose was expressed in the Sinai covenant. Upon Israel, in the divine intent, Yahweh conferred the status of "a kingdom of priests and a holy nation."[8] However crude their moral and spiritual insight, Israel had been elected to help fulfill God's supreme purpose in history. As no other nation, Israel became a people with a mission. All their subsequent history was to be crucial to the fulfillment of that mission. Thus purposeful, their national existence acquired historical significance, bound as no other people both to make history and to write history. Divine-human historiography would become the intellectual counterpart of their fervent religious commitment, even though Israel repeatedly broke the commitment.

There had been other migrations, *Völkerwanderungen,* divinely led. Amos argues to that effect when as God's spokesman he writes, "Did I [God] not bring up Israel from the land of Egypt, and the Philistines from Caphtor [Crete] and the Syrians from Kir?"[9] It was the conviction of Amos that a divine providence operates in behalf of all peoples. According to him, God, as the universal Judge, has all nations under His jurisdiction as well as under His providence. All nations are confronted by Him in love and in judgment.

Amos. As a prophet of God Amos believed that all nations were confronted by Him in both love and judgment. Engraving by Gustave Doré. Historical Pictures Service, Chicago.

Many nations there were, but only Israel was elected by God for this one transcendent purpose. Yet there is no inconsistency in Amos's message. Israel's overconfidence in its privileged position compelled the prophet to stress God's concern for all nations. Israel's privilege bred her conceit.

When on another occasion Amos must underscore Israel's dereliction, he grounds his indictment on the historical events of the Exodus and the covenant, "Hear this word that the Lord has spoken against you, O people of Israel, against the whole family which I brought up out of the land of Egypt: 'You only have I known of all the families of the earth; therefore I will punish you for all your iniquities.' "[10] In prophetic parlance "to know" meant that Israel alone had become an object of God's special concern. God is concerned with all nations, as Amos himself states in chapters 1 and 2, but His concern for Israel had a unique dimension, a specific responsibility.

Amos exerted considerable influence upon his younger contemporary Hosea, as well as upon all subsequent Biblical writers. A tabulation of Amos's basic historical presuppositions might look something as follows:

1. All nations stand under divine judgment. Amos 1 and 2.[11]

2. Israel as the most favored nation stands under greatest responsibility. Amos 3:2.[12]

3. God is active not only in history but also in nature. The series of natural calamities which had befallen Israel (listed in Amos 4) were interpreted as divine judgments. The first two visions of chapter 7 illustrate the same point. Nature is the handmaid of God who is likewise the Lord of history.

4. The world is a world of law. This principle (chapter 3:3-5), although obvious to modern man steeped in the scientific tradition of the last three centuries, represented a remarkable insight in an age of empiriological thinking.

5. Rite is no substitute for right. Ritual punctiliousness can never take the place of righteous living and social justice (chapter 5, verses 21-24).

How well Israel measured up or failed to measure up to her moral responsibility under the covenant is the main theme of the historical books of the Old Testament. The writers are strikingly candid in admitting over and again that the people Israel, particularly their kings, failed dismally in their divinely appointed mission. That national pride did not interfere with historical objectivity is nothing short of miraculous. The Old Testament stands in sharp contrast to the annals of the Assyrian kings, which consistently magnify the victories and gloss over the defeats. There is no attempt in the record to cover up Israel's failure before the bar of world opinion. First the kingdom of the North (the ten tribes) and then that of the South (Judah and Benjamin) are taken to task for their disloyalty to the Sinaitic covenant. God did not fail, but the nation repeatedly failed in meeting its spiritual obligations under the covenant relationship. If the nation should be restored after the Exile, then the restoration would have to be an act of pure divine grace. That the nation was partially restored after the Babylonian captivity placed upon it a double obligation of gratitude: first to divine election and second to divine forgiveness.

It is remarkable that a consecutive narrative of Israel's history from the Exodus to the Exile, a span of about a millennium, was even preserved. This also stands in telling contrast to the paucity or sometimes total absence of historical data for most of the neighboring peoples. What accounts for the difference is that history to Israel was full of meaning. It was the unfolding record of national election and mission rather than just another bombastic chronicle.

The book of Judges implies that after the earth-shaking Exodus, which galvanized the national conscience and brought to the forefront such charismatic leaders as Moses and Joshua, Israel drifted into a dark age.[13] A parallel to this is found in the dark age which fell upon Greece after the days of Mycenaean splendor, or upon western Europe following the ephemeral resurgence under Charlemagne. It was a time when, as the record states, "every man did what was right in his own eyes."[14] But the centrifugal forces which tended to break up the nation into so many tribes, each shifting for itself, were counteracted by the centripetal memory of their common experience in the period of the conquest and of the covenant renewal under Joshua. Moreover the community of tradition was reinforced by loyalty to a central shrine where Yahweh's invisible presence was honored. As long as the sanctuary in Shilo stood as a bulwark against encroaching Baal worship, some faith in the continuing presence of Yahweh still persisted.

The epic poem of Deborah marks the best and perhaps the most instructive section of the book of Judges.[15] There are other heroic accounts in this book, such as those of Gideon, Jephthah, and Samson; but in none of these does the national spirit rise to such a level as in the episode immortalized by the poetry of Deborah.

The epic opens with a word of thanksgiving to Yahweh, followed by a rhetorical summons to kings and princes to listen to the song which is dedicated to Yahweh, "the God of Israel." This is followed by a historical prologue linking the present crisis in national life to Yahweh's theophany on Sinai where the nation had its birth. A description of the gloomy conditions prevailing in the country in the days of Shamgar is logically connected to the apostasy which was the undoing of so many in Israel "when new gods were chosen."[16]

The rest of the poem shares the conviction that a repentant nation, rallying around its leaders to defend the commonwealth, can depend on God's blessings and victory. Victory was never assumed to be a human achievement per se, but on the other hand the importance of human cooperation with the divine purpose is never disparaged. In fact, if one virtue is praised in the poem more than others, it is that of willing cooperation on man's part.[17]

Even in the low ebb of Israel's experience as a nation the poem of Deborah shows that the nation never lost its historical awareness. It continued to have history because the conviction that national existence played a role in the divine scheme was never fully lost.[18]

The books of Samuel, particularly the second book, shine as a morning bright with hope after a gloomy night. Israelite historiography reaches its high mark in the court annals of David, as recorded in 2 Samuel 9 to 20 and 1 Kings 1 and 2. O. Eissfeldt in his *Introduction to the Old Testament* points out the remarkable contrast between the historical documents of the Assyrians and Babylonians, Egyptians and Hittites, in which the "I" narratives predominate, and the total absence of such stylistic form in the historical sections of the Old Testament.[19] Building inscriptions from every site in other nations are as a rule in the "I" narrative style, whereas the only building inscription ever found in Israelite Palestine, namely, the Siloam Inscription, does not even mention the name of the king, Hezekiah.[20]

The explanation of this notable feature demonstrates again that Biblical historiography is theocentric, God-centered, rather than king-centered. Outstanding personalities such as Abraham, Moses, Samuel, and David arise from time to time; but their national prominence is never conceived as self-grounded. Whatever great they accomplished on the stage of history, they did as instruments of the divine will. Whether reminiscing the minor exploits of a Gideon or a Jephthah, or the more lasting achievements of David or Hezekiah, the focus of attention is not on men, but on God, who stirs His servants to heroic deeds. In this sense Yahweh is the only hero of the Old Testament.

Even supposing that some of these charismatic leaders left autobiographies, a common practice for many Egyptian noblemen, the incorporation of such "I" narratives in the Biblical record would offend the religious conscience. In consequence, the deeply rooted conviction that all glory belongs to God pervades every piece of historical composition. A singular exception to this rule is Nehemiah, who in his memoirs draws much attention to his individual accomplishments. But Nehemiah's memoirs, dating from the latter part of the fifth century B.C., belong to the last phase of Biblical historiography. His self-laudatory homilies seem less harsh in view of the fact that his motives were constantly called into question by detractors.

If Amos stressed the universal justice of God, "Let justice roll down like waters, and righteousness like an ever-flowing stream,"[21] his contemporary Hosea exalted divine mercy. This insight into God's nature, rooted as it was in the tragic experience of his domestic life, was the necessary counterpart to Amos's stern message, which left seemingly little hope to a derelict nation. The inevitable tension between the demand for national and individual righteousness and the equally important truth of divine love which cannot let the sinner go, is never fully resolved until the cross, where "mercy and truth . . . met together."[22] Yet prophets like Isaiah and Jeremiah hold before a recreant people the prospect of forgiveness and restoration conditioned on repentance, literally a turning back to God. While no cheap pardon is proffered, no sinner remains unforgiven if he comes to God with a broken and contrite heart.[23]

Habakkuk offers an interesting bit of philosophy in an age not particularly noted for philosophers—at least two centuries before Plato.

His challenging little book opens with a controversy on the justice of God's dealings with men. In his first address to God the prophet complains that injustice flaunts its impudent head in high places. In reply God assures the prophet that He is rousing the Chaldeans to punish wickedness wherever found. But far from quieting Habakkuk's fears, the disclosure of a coming judgment provokes another complaint. Where is justice if God uses the wicked to swallow up "the man more righteous than he?"[24] Why should God consider those who idolized power—the Chaldeans—to be less guilty than those who perverted justice—the Jews?

Armed with his seemingly invulnerable argument, the prophet assumes a posture of expectancy tinged with conceit. In the next scene the Lord appears to him to reiterate that the vision of impending punishment of the wicked is sure, though slow. To this is added a rebuke to the prophet himself for his conceit.

"Behold," God tells him, "he whose soul is not upright in him is puffed up [margin], but the righteous shall live by his faith."[25] Habakkuk was evidently puffed up with his self-supposed ability to puncture holes in God's designs. His limited flight into the thin air of the rationale of history, though not to be discouraged, must not be allowed to degenerate into presumption. Man's finest insights fall ever short of the whole truth. Unaided reason must never presume to outwit faith.

Even the least promising sections of the Old Testament, such as the genealogical lists interspersed here and there, may yield profound spiritual insights to the sympathetic reader. G. von Rad remarks that these genealogical lists constitute by their very monotony "a profound expression of the knowledge of a saving relationship between God and His people which is unchanged from the very beginning."[26]

The Old Testament is one great witness to God's redeeming activity, first in the history of Israel as the chosen nation, and second in the history of all nations. History is purposeful and is moving toward a goal of God's own choice, a glorious consummation to be reached in "the day of the Lord." Setbacks resulting from apostasy would not stop it. Even though, as it eventually became clear, the nation would have to pass through the fiery ordeal of exile to remove the dross from the gold, a resolute faith in God's *chesed, i.e.,* divine loyalty to the covenant made with the fathers, allied with a compelling sense of mission, would nevertheless allow a faithful remnant to see meaning even in history's darkest hour.

NOTES AND REFERENCES

1. See Exodus 19:5, 6; Ezekiel 37:26-28.
2. C. R. North, *The Old Testament Interpretation of History,* page 143.
3. G. von Rad, *Old Testament Theology,* Vol. 1, tr., p. 106.
4. G. Ernest Wright, *God Who Acts,* page 44.
5. Psalm 53:3.
6. Hosea 11:8.
7. Cf. John Gray, *The KRT Text in the Literature of Ras Shamra.* Leiden: E. J. Brill, 1955.
8. Exodus 19:6.
9. Amos 9:7.
10. Amos 3:1, 2.
11. The validity of this assumption is not diminished even if the list of foreign nations is reduced from six to four, as some critics would have it.
12. This agrees with the saying of Jesus, "Everyone to whom much is given, of him will much be required." Luke 12:48.
13. What is known of this dark age of Israel's past is not entirely due to oral traditions put into writing at a much later date. The Song of Deborah (Judges 5) with its many archaic features, as shown by Albright and others, points to a date contemporaneous with the events described, namely, c. 1125 B.C. See W. F. Albright in *Old Testament and Modern Study* (Oxford Clarendon Press, 1951), page 33.
14. Judges 21:25.
15. For a recent appraisal of the "Song of Deborah," see Eric Voegelin, *Order and History,* I (Louisiana State University Press, 1956), pages 199 ff.
16. This bit of moral judgment, being as it is an integral part of the poem, deflates considerably the argument that the moralizing portions of the historical books come from the Deuteronomist circle, and were superimposed on the original unobtrusive narrative. Closer to the truth is that Deborah shared with all inspired writers the conviction that apostasy, as a breach of the covenant, could only entail divine displeasure.
17. Judges 5:2, 9, 13, 18.
18. The date of Deborah's poem proposed by Albright is substantiated by the fact that writing was widely practiced in the Canaanite milieu, as attested by the findings in Ugarit of a slightly older date, or by the Gezer Calendar (c. 1200 B.C.).
19. See O. Eissfeldt, *Einleitung in das Alte Testament* (Tübingen: J. C. B. Mohr, 1964), pages 66 ff.
20. See J. B. Pritchard (ed.), *Ancient Near Eastern Texts,* page 321.
21. Amos 5:24.
22. Psalm 85:10, KJV.
23. Psalm 51:17.
24. Habbakuk 1:13.
25. Habbakuk 2:4. The RSV translator obviously misunderstood the force of the dialogue, and substituted the Hebrew "is puffed up" by the pointless "shall fail."
26. G. von Rad, *Das Geschicktbild des chronistischen Werkes* (1930), page 66, quoted in W. Eichrodt, *Theology of the Old Testament,* Vol. 1, p. 64.

Chapter 5

Paul's View of History

As the most articulate spokesman of the early Christian faith to the Gentile world, Paul, as he expounded the gospel, could not avoid touching on history. That God is active in history is one of the basic assumptions of his *kerygma,* or message. God, who had of old spoken "in many and various ways" to the fathers, had now made His will known to man by His Son.[1] This divine disclosure occurred not to some mystic seer in some remote corner, but under very strictly defined historical circumstances.

Through Paul's writings shines his conviction of a redemptive purpose at work in history, a purpose only dimly apprehended in Old Testament times but now clearly seen by men in the incarnation of Jesus Christ. All the adumbrations seen in sacrifices, temple ritual, and prophecies had in "the fullness of time"[2] met their reality in Christ. A new era had dawned for mankind when Jesus Christ crossed over the threshold into human history. The preparatory school of the law and the prophets had achieved its goal by introducing the One in whom "all the fullness of God was pleased to dwell."[3]

How did the Gentiles fit into the wider, brighter scheme envisaged by the gospel? Was their inclusion in the plan of redemption an afterthought, or was it all the while grounded in God's eternal plan? These and related questions pressed for an answer, and the apostle, under divine inspiration, had the explanation.

Paul's first recorded address to pagans on the subject of God's relation to Gentiles was delivered at Lystra.[4] To dissuade his zealous admirers from offering divine honors to him and Barnabas after a miraculous healing, Paul insisted that they were only common humans and challenged the people to "turn from these vain things [pagan superstitions] to a living God who made the heaven and the earth and the sea and all that is in them." God, Paul told them, is Creator. Rather than bowing down before idols, man's creation, they should bow down to the Creator of all. Men of all nations must honor this living God, since He is the Creator of them all.

Less obvious to his Gentile audience was the reason this good news had remained concealed for so long. Paul anticipated this unspoken objection in his next statement. "In past generations He allowed all the nations to walk in their own ways." In Paul's view God had permitted man's age-long quest after the divine to follow its own course like a river meandering at the bottom of a valley. No worldwide constraint had been brought to bear upon man's conscience compelling him to acknowledge a divine rulership. Evidently it served some transcendent good that man should be left to grope after God with a minimum of guidance. Intimations of God's lordship over nature and history were there to behold, but they were never so overwhelming that man could not question their cogency if he chose to do so.

"Yet," Paul continued, "He did not leave Himself without witness." Even though God was "the unknown God," not only in Athens but throughout the pagan world, there was nevertheless no final alibi for universal ignorance. Evidence of a kind and gracious God had always been available, "for He did good and gave you from heaven rains and fruitful seasons, satisfying your hearts with food and gladness." To the common man of Lystra Paul pointed out God's providences in nature as witnesses to His existence and love. This made sense to him.[5] Nature had often been misinterpreted, and its variegated manifestations may even have fostered belief in a multitude of gods. But there was no intrinsic ambiguity in nature that would of necessity lead to misinterpretation. God's bounty had provided man with "rains and fruitful seasons, satisfying your hearts with food and gladness."

The theme of his address at Lystra, "In past generations He allowed all nations to walk in their own ways," Paul would pursue on future occasions. Later, when the apostle was haled before the Areopagus to explain to the novelty-enthralled Athenians the substance of the new "good news" sweeping the world, he stressed the following points as recorded in Acts 17:

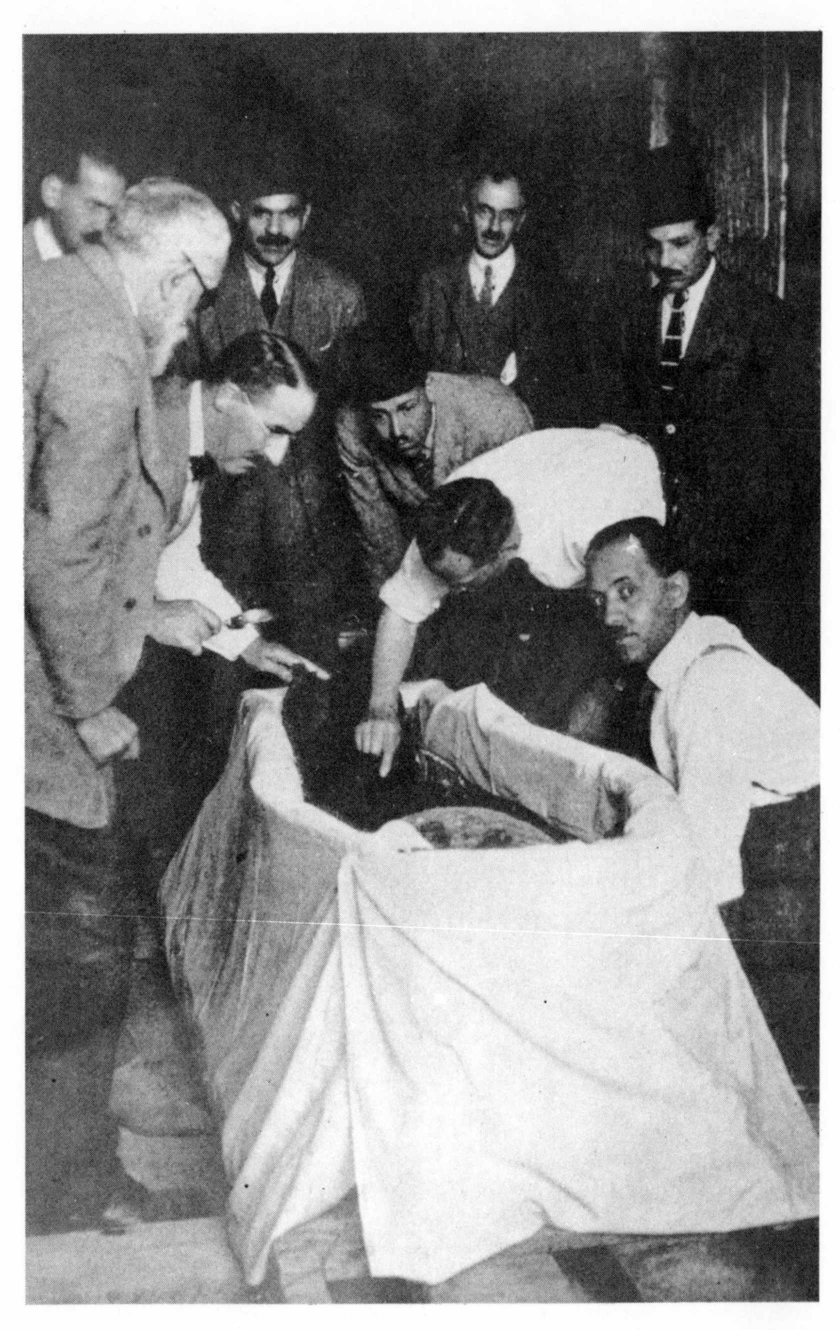

Egyptologists open coffin of Tutankhamen (King Tut) in 1922. Monotheism might have fared better in ancient Egypt had this young king lived and continued the policies of his predecessor, Ikhnaton. Historical Pictures Service, Chicago.

1. The "unknown God" whom Paul proclaimed is no other than the Creator of all things. Verse 24.

2. His rule is universal, embracing heaven and earth. Verse 24.

3. This universal God is not dependent on human service for comfort and welfare. Deeply ingrained in the pagan mind was the notion that man was charged with sustaining the gods as servants would sustain a king. In its quaint way the Babylonian "Epic of Creation" tells that mankind was created to be "charged with the service that the gods may then have rest."[6] On the contrary, says Paul, God is not "served by human hands, as though he needed anything," but rather mankind is dependent on God for breath and life and "everything." Verse 25.

4. All nations share a common humanity as creatures of the one God. Verse 26.

5. Nations are assigned definite boundaries in time and space within which to fulfill their destiny. Verse 27.

6. The chief goal of national and individual existence is a religious one—"that they might feel after Him [God] and find Him." Verse 27.

After arguing why this goal was not beyond human reach (verses 28, 29), Paul returns to the theme which must have preoccupied every reflective listener. Would men and nations be held accountable for the neglected opportunities of the past? Paul's answer is unequivocal, "The times of ignorance God overlooked." Verse 30.

Paul was probably acutely aware of the religious speculations of the peoples of Mesopotamia which led them to an ever-deepening morass of superstition and obscurantism. They might have known God. The possibility had been there all along. But for all their groping after light, they seemed to drift farther and farther into darkness.

The picture presented by Egyptian religion was no brighter. Despite the once-promising glimmer in the days of Ikhnaton when man's search for truth took a turn toward the idea of one god, rank polytheism held Egyptian thought in thrall from beginning to end. The power-conscious priests of Amen in Thebes bear chief responsibility for crushing the budding religious aspirations of the Amarna Age. Despite the dazzling funeral gifts which adorned the tomb of young Tutankhamen, successor to Ikhnaton, his name was expunged from the canon of the kings, perhaps because of his association with his unorthodox predecessor. By stifling the monotheistic aspirations of Ikhnaton and promoting the muddled superstitions of the past, the priests of Amen saddled the New Kingdom with a system of gross paganism.

On the other hand some evidence does exist showing that God's "allotted periods" were not entirely barren of spiritual fruitage. In Persia, in the seventh century B.C., Zoroaster distinguished himself by remarkable insights into religious truth. He replaced the contradictory claims of Iranian polytheism by belief in Ahura Mazda, the god of truth and light, who is opposed by the evil spirit Angra Mainyu. Zoroastrianism recognizes a protracted struggle in which the forces of good eventually prevail. The notion of a final judgment emerges with the prospect of eternal life for those who side with Ahura Mazda. The god of Zoroaster is conceived as a spiritual deity of whom the best representation was fire. No temples are to be erected, since nature itself is God's most glorious temple. There are glimpses of truth in Zoroaster's religious intuitions, dim reflections of "the true light that enlightens every man."[7]

The same century that witnessed the teaching of Zoroaster in Persia saw the reforming activities of Guatama in India. This teacher aimed at redeeming Hinduism from its more objectionable features, particularly its bent toward the proliferation of gods. India had its opportunity of embracing a purer faith but allowed its opportunity to slip by, while Buddhism itself eventually sank into passive contemplation. Almost contemporaneously Confucius was introducing the ferment of his moralistic teaching into Chinese society. Though not grounding his ethics upon any clear religious conviction, Confucius belonged nevertheless to the same tradition as the seventh-century Hebrew prophets who in their preaching also stressed that life must be shaped by the awareness of moral duty.

Paul's statement that God is willing to overlook "the times of ignorance," does not imply that all past Gentile history was totally devoid of moral and religious worth. All he implies is that mankind fell far short of the divine goal set for it. This is made clearer when Paul returns to the theme in the first paragraphs of his letter to the Romans, easily the fullest treatment of the subject from his pen.

Beginning with verse 19 of Romans 1 Paul, in the following points, sets the Gentile world within the divine scheme:

1. God had disclosed Himself to the Gentiles in terms clear enough to be grasped if they cared to examine the evidence. Verse 19.

2. God's self-disclosure is best seen by His creative power shown in nature. Verse 20.

3. Mankind started with a knowledge of God but lost it through pride and perverted reasoning. Verse 21.

4. Sinful pride had such a depraving influence upon the intellect that, leaving a knowledge of the true God, man ended in crass polytheism. Verses 22, 23.

5. Divinity allowed man to reap the full result of his willful blindness which issued into the grossest immorality. Verses 24-32.

6. Thus man stands without an excuse before God. Romans 1:20; 2:1.

7. Yet a dim residual knowledge of God's will remained stamped upon man's conscience. Despite sin's devastating effects God's image in man was not completely obliterated. Verses 12-14.

8. And finally, man will be judged according to his response to the inner light of conscience which was never entirely extinguished either. Verses 15, 16.

In the light of these premises Paul offered to his Gentile readers a consistent theodicy. God's way of dealing with the non-Jews appeared justified. True, the Gentiles had enjoyed less light than the Jews, who had been "entrusted with the oracles of God,"[8] namely, a written revelation. Nevertheless the pagan world was "without excuse," since God never abandoned it to utter darkness. Palpable evidence of God's creatorship was present in nature for those willing to recognize it. If the world at large ignored that evidence, no blame attached to God.

Paul's teaching that God assigned different nations "boundaries of their habitation," is firmly rooted in Jewish tradition and may be traced to the "song" ascribed to Moses in Deuteronomy: "When the Most High gave to the nations their inheritance, when He separated the sons of man, He fixed the bounds of the peoples."[9]

Paul adds that not only geographical bounds but also "allotted periods" were assigned to each by God's design. He must have been acquainted with the fact that nations and empires had appeared on the world stage, played their role with greater or lesser splendor, only to sink back into oblivion. Was there any reason for this recurring drama? Under diverse symbols Daniel in his apocalypse had portrayed four world empires which succeeded each other on the stage of history. Each had its "allotted time" and had basked for a while in the noontide of world dominion, only to relinquish in due course the supremacy to a greater power.

Philosophers of history probe into the causes of the death of civilizations. With the meager record before them they are expected to make a postmortem investigation of each case and present a convincing coroner's report. Political and military factors were fashionable villains in older case studies. Since Karl Marx the fad is to assign economic reasons a major role in the rise and collapse of civilizations.

In his *Decline of the West,* O. Spengler regards the death of a civilization as natural as the death of a biological specimen. Both run their anticipated life cycle, nothing more, nothing less. According to A. Toynbee death comes to a civilization when its creative minority ceases to inspire the mimicking majority with its own worth. When the leading minority becomes a dominant clique, when its ability to inspire is replaced by the urge to exploit, there occurs a "secession of the proletariat," which is the first symptom of disintegration. The internal proletariat, viz., the urban masses, then turn for guidance to false messiahs, as a rule political demagogues, while the external proletariat, viz., the barbarian hordes beyond the frontiers kept in check by the awe-inspiring superior civilization, exchange their admiration for spite. This secession in the body politic leads consequently to a loss of self-determination, which is "the ultimate criterion of breakdown."[10]

No single explanation of the breakdown of civilizations has received what even approaches a consensus of opinion. The mechanism is too complex to be reduced to a single formula. What seems plausible in one instance is far from plausible in others. Toynbee's analysis has the merit of transferring the problem from a purely materialistic level, where the variables are environmental or military or economic, to a more typically human spiritual level, where the gain or loss of self-determination is the ultimate criterion of growth or breakdown.

Paul raises the problem yet higher, to the level of religious decision. Each nation is assigned a limited opportunity to attune its political existence to God's eternal order, presupposing that a nation perfectly attuned with God would remain forever.

Foreglimpses of this interpretation are traceable to the prophetic writings of the Old Testament. Israel was meant to enjoy this status, to become the nucleus around which all nations would revolve in the divine order. Ezekiel voiced this concept in these words: "This is Jerusalem; I have set her in the center of the nations, with countries round about her."[11] Thus strategically located in the divine intent, Israel was to become the creative minority which would lead the surrounding nations to acknowledge the only true God. But Israel fell short, its appointed time running out when it failed to recognize the Messiah. And yet to the incipient Christian church the miscarriage of divine election never ceased to be a source of perplexity.

Paul tackles this thorny problem, opening (Romans 9) with the apparent arbitrariness of divine election, an aspect most likely to trouble his Gentile readers. His argument boils down to this: God is free in the exercise of His mercy. "He has mercy upon whomever he wills."[12] Mercy, by its very nature, is under obligation to no one. Whereas justice is of necessity bound to law, even if that law is no other than God's holy will, mercy is absolutely free. The election of Israel, which cannot be accounted for on the basis of justice, is perfectly agreeable on the basis of mercy. "I will have mercy," declared the Lord to Moses, "on whom I have mercy, and I will have compassion on whom I have compassion."[13]

Israel's election was an act of grace. In Paul's terminology mercy is evidently synonymous with grace. No distinction can be drawn between the "mercy" of chapter 9 and the "grace" of chapter 11. Israel, then, like the remnant, was "chosen by grace."[14] But its continuance in grace was made conditional on faith, a faith which must be understood as a loving, trusting relationship between the believer and the One who made the promise.

This was the stumbling block. Israel chosen by grace wanted to make a claim on God on the basis of merit, her own righteousness. "But," argues Paul, "if it is by grace, it is no longer on the basis of works; otherwise grace would no longer be grace."[15] To the last Israel strove blindly to retain "chosen nation" status on the basis of merit, thus undermining the very ground of that choice, pure grace. The Pharisees had misread the nation's past. They knew about Abraham's call, but they understood little of that experience of trusting fellowship with the Eternal which made Abraham "father of the believers." They could quote the covenant which at Sinai set the nation aside as a "holy nation." But they little realized that the covenant was grounded, not on the nation's greatness or goodness, but on God's grace, and that continuance in grace was dependent not on legal righteousness, but on the obedience that springs out of loving communion. The key concept of covenant loyalty, so important to the prophets, was grossly misunderstood as requiring legalistic punctiliousness. The personal religion of the patriarchs had hardened into a perfunctory round of ritual and law. The typical Pharisee erected the law as a barrier between himself and his God. He preferred, so to speak, to be confronted by God on the basis of law rather than on the basis of love, thus missing the very heart of his own religion.

Attempting the impossible, viz., to establish a claim upon God on grounds of her own righteousness, Israel forfeited her status as a "chosen nation" by refusing to respond in faith and by renouncing grace or mercy, the very foundation of election. When in the fullness of time Christ presented God's claim on the nation as His peculiar people, Israel rejected the claim by declaring before Pilate, "We have no king but Caesar!"[16] The same people which so gallantly resisted the Hellenistic threat to its religious stance in the days of Judas Maccabaeus, now failed miserably to recognize the Messiah for whose advent the nation had been chosen in the first place. By rejecting the One for whom the nation was elected by God, Israel rejected the election itself.

Yet the rejection was not total, because there was still a remnant "chosen by grace."[17] Paul numbered himself among this remnant. Nor was the rejection final. "Even the others," says Paul, although broken off the mystical olive tree because of unbelief, "if they do not persist in their unbelief, will be grafted in."[18] The possibility of restoration remained for the individual believer who alone can make the response of faith to divine grace.

A. Nygren denies that Paul is here engaged in presenting his philosophy of history.[19] While granting that Paul's primary interest is theological and not philosophical, and that in the context of Romans the problem of the rejection of Israel looms larger than Israel's peculiar role in the *historia mundi,* it remains nevertheless true that the apostle cannot disengage the theological question from its historical implications. Israel's historical destiny was only partially fulfilled, and her dereliction created hardship for, and imposed new obligations upon, the nascent Christian church.

Paul continues his philosophy of history in his letter to the Ephesians, which John A. Mackay terms "the greatest and maturest of all his writings."[20] Nygren's *caveat* or caution that Paul's concern is primarily theological and only secondarily historical is just as applicable to Ephesians as to Romans. Yet no disquisition on the Christian faith with such firm rootage in history can possibly escape history.

In contrast to myth, whose connection with history is merely accidental, the Christian faith is involved in the drama of redemption enacted on the very stage of history. The historical frame is not an accessory which can be ignored in some so-called "deeper" level of understanding. Ephesians not only shares this characteristic with other New Testament writings, but exhibits it in an even bolder light.

Echoing through the epistle as a musical refrain is the proclamation of a divine purpose "to unite all things in Him [Christ], things in heaven and things on earth."[21] This plan to reunite "all things" in Christ presumes a rift in the fabric of the universe. As Mackay puts it, "History and the heart of man are rifted. The fact of a rift is the elemental, decisive fact about reality in its wholeness."[22] The state of the moral universe is not at present, according to Paul, what God intended it to be. The stark fact of sin introduced spiritual disorder into the cosmos. Disharmony invaded both the heavenly and the earthly spheres.

In regard to the supramundane realm Paul somberly refers to "spiritual hosts of wickedness in the heavenly places."[23] God's sovereignty in the universe He created is challenged. The dualism Paul alludes to is not absolute, though painfully real. The source of evil is creaturely, finite, and yet like some infectious disease which must run its course before the physician can intervene effectively, evil must run its course before final eradication.

Consequently a conflict rages in the moral universe causing repercussions from which none is immune. The reality of sin, the spiritual rift of cosmic dimension, is one of the basic presuppositions of the Scriptures. God's forbearance in dealing with this disaffection in every level, individual, social, and cosmic, is the dominant Biblical concern. There is never a doubt that God's order will ultimately prevail. Unity will be restored. The cacophonous dissonances of the present will at last give place to universal adoration. Until then, right will be often on the scaffold, wrong often on the throne.

According to Ephesians the divine plan to heal the rift caused by sin was laid "before the foundation of the world."[24] But full disclosure of its glorious scope was made only now, when the mystery of redemptive love became an open secret, as it was "revealed to His holy apostles and prophets by the Spirit."[25] But its inception lay in eternity hidden in divine foreknowledge.

For the individual believer the mystery meant first of all the good news of redemption through the blood of Christ, the forgiveness of sin "according to the riches of His grace."[26] Man dead through trespasses, "alienated from the life of God,"[27] allured by "the desires of body and mind," enchained by the propensities of his lower nature, experienced redemption as the galvanizing power of a new life, as a veritable resurrection from the dead. The bonds of sin broken, man in his new freedom felt like a new creature catapulted to "the heavenly places in Christ Jesus."[28] By His ineffable grace God offered man the gift of salvation, and through faith man appropriated it. This, in brief, was the effect of the divine-human encounter which healed the vertical rift in the microcosm of individual existence.

But beyond unity lies community as an integral part of the gospel of reconciliation. Men reconciled with God enter into a new relationship with their fellowmen. The deep-seated hostility engendered by sin which alienates man from his fellows, and nations from each other, is now vanquished by love radiating from the cross of Christ. Jews and Gentiles are both reconciled "to God in one body through the cross, thereby bringing the hostility to an end."[29] Man through self-love had erected a "dividing wall of hostility"[30] between himself and his fellow creatures. Greed and exploitation had placed the "have-nots" against the "haves." Walls had separated civilized countries from the "underdeveloped" barbarians beyond the border. Yet nowhere was the natural hostility brought into sharper focus than between the "chosen" few and the "outcast" Gentiles beyond the pale. Here, where hostility was most patently self-defeating, it assumed its most sinister mood. Religion-inspired enmity reveals the breach of sin in its most tragic dimension.

The lonely cross on Golgotha was heaven's remedy for healing both the rift alienating man from God, and the rift separating man from his fellows. After the Christ event the Gentile world could unite with the "commonwealth of Israel," because through Christ we all "have access in one Spirit to the Father." Paul envisages nothing less than a new humanity, world-embracing in extent, the components of which are all "fellow citizens with the saints and members of the household of God."[31]

To achieve this world community it pleased God to use the church, through which "the manifold wisdom of God"[32] is made known to intelligent beings both in heaven and on earth. The living church becomes the symbol and pledge of God's will to unity, the nucleus around which a society in the process of dissolution recrystallizes into a community reflecting God's eternal order. The divine strategy requires that the church become the rallying point for all men of goodwill. Through the church, then, as the body of Christ, fully equipped with the gifts of the Spirit to carry out its mission of conciliation, is God's redeeming purpose to be finally realized.

NOTES AND REFERENCES

1. Hebrews 1:1, 2.
2. Galatians 4:4.
3. Colossians 1:19.
4. Acts 14:15-17.
5. Refreshingly, Paul did not here single out some abstruse evidence of God's existence in the speculations of philosophers and sages, though this is not to imply that to Paul's mind nothing could be learned about God in the "dialogues" of Plato or the "logic" of Aristotle. In fact, in another context (Acts 17:28), and before a more sophisticated audience, Paul would quote poets Aratus and Epimenides, whose writings contained some inklings of divine truth.
6. See J. B. Pritchard, ed., *Ancient Near Eastern Texts Relating to the Old Testament,* page 68. Quotation translated from cuneiform by the Old Society for Old Testament Study in D. Winton Thomas (ed.), *Documents From Old Testament Times,* page 12.
7. John 1:9.
8. Romans 3:2.
9. Deuteronomy 32:8.
10. A. Toynbee, *A Study of History,* abrgd. by D. C. Somervell, pages 275-279.
11. Ezekiel 5:5.
12. Romans 9:18.
13. Romans 9:15.
14. Romans 11:5.

15. Romans 11:6.
16. John 19:15.
17. Romans 11:5.
18. Romans 11:23. See also verse 24.
19. A. Nygren, *Commentary on Romans,* tr., page 355.
20. John A. Mackay, *God's Order,* page ix. The Pauline authorship of Ephesians is denied by Feine, Behm and Kummel in their *Introduction to the New Testament,* tr., pages 247-258, but reaffirmed by R. M. Grant, *A Historical Introduction to the New Testament,* pages 199 ff. There are able scholars on both sides of the issue, which shows how difficult it is to reach a decision on purely internal evidence. The author is greatly indebted for this portion of the chapter to John Mackay's enlightening exposition.
21. Ephesians 1:10.
22. John A. Mackay, *op. cit.,* p. 25.
23. Ephesians 6:12.
24. Ephesians 1:4.
25. Ephesians 3:5.
26. Ephesians 1:7.
27. Ephesians 4:18.
28. See Ephesians 2:1-6.
29. Ephesians 2:16.
30. Ephesians 2:14.
31. Ephesians 2:11, 18, 19.
32. Ephesians 3:10.

Chapter 6

The Burden of Egypt

How did Egypt measure up to its opportunity to seek God, "in the hope that they might feel after Him and find Him"?[1]

No other civilization enjoyed such a long period of grace as did the enduring civilization of the Nile Valley. For over two thousand years its unperturbed splendor struck awe upon the surrounding nations. Even in its decaying stage, when the penetrating eyes of an Isaiah could perceive the broken reed disguised under a pretense of ancient might, the petty nations of western Asia sought its protection from the terrifying Assyrian scourge. If the heyday of its military strength was to be found during the Eighteenth Dynasty, c. 1450 B.C., then its descent to the netherworld, to use the grim imagery of Ezekiel 32, was as languid as a funeral procession.

Within the context of the Biblical philosophy of religion, the rise and fall of the empire by the Nile was not important. Nor was the confused picture of Egyptian religion. What was ultimately important to Egypt was her spiritual pilgrimage—how she made use of her opportunity to seek after God within the time span granted to her. In a civilization which to the superficial eye seems static in every aspect, where the canons of art and protocol, the concepts of religion and political administration, appear to have been fixed from the earliest days, the very idea of a spiritual pilgrimage seems preposterous. A careful sifting of the evidence will show, however, that not everything was settled once for all time. Egypt had its times of trouble when men's souls were tried and religious complacency was shaken to the very roots.

One of the most striking documents portraying Egyptian religious concepts is the Shabaka Stone dating from 700 B.C. Internal evidence points to its derivation from a text composed early in the Old Kingdom when Memphis became the capital of the empire. Budge, discussing this episode, says that the priests of the god Ptah, whose abode was in Memphis, rose under royal stimulus "to the highest conception of God which was ever reached in Egypt, and their religion was a pure monotheism. They evolved the idea of God as a Spirit, a self-created, self-subsisting, eternal, almighty mind-god, who created everything that is merely by thinking."[2] Or, quoting the translation of the text by John A. Wilson, "Indeed, all the divine order really came into being through what the heart thought and the tongue commanded."[3] Thus at the very outset of its recorded history the Egyptian mind grasped the concept of a divine logos not far removed from that found in John 1:1: "In the beginning was the Word, and the Word was with God, and the Word was God."

It is not unthinkable to ascribe the wonderful creativity of the Egyptian mind under the Third and Fourth Dynasties to such a lofty conception of deity. Artistic genius soared to the purest height. During the reign of Djoser the architect Imhotep mastered the technical problems involved in the erection of the first mastaba pyramid. Skill in mathematical computation was never surpassed in subsequent generations. From this age, too, comes the "Edwin Smith Surgical Papyrus," justly admired for its scientific outlook. The daring of the engineers who built the pyramids of Cheops, Khefren, and Mykerinos vividly illustrates the zest for action and accomplishment which characterized this period—great in many ways. In one bold stroke, it seems, Egyptian creativity reached its zenith, establishing standards of excellence which became normative for all subsequent ages.

The flash of insight of the priests of Ptah, which conceived creation as an act of thought, was also worthy of the pyramid age. But apparently that high concept never filtered down to the common people, who remained steeped in the superstitions of polytheism inherited from the predynastic days. Some reflective souls may even have considered the sun, the moon, and the other powers of nature as manifestations of one supreme god. But to the masses Ra, visible in the sun, continued to make his voyage across the sky in his solar bark. The earth was the god Geb, and the wind was deified as Shu. The ram-headed god Khnum retained in popular superstition the role of creator who fashioned men's bodies on a potter's wheel. The underworld was ruled by Osiris with his consort Isis. The tendency to group the gods in triads made Osiris and Isis the progenitors of the falcon-headed Horus, of whom the living pharaoh was believed to be an incarnation.

Besides the cosmic deities[4] which enjoyed nationwide prestige, there were the local deities worshipped in different nomes. Of these, some were conceived as animals such as the crocodile-god Sobekh or the lion-goddess Sekhmet. Others were thought of as having a human body with an animal head such as Thoth with an ibis head. A few, like Osiris, were thought to be purely human in form.

Important to the Biblical philosophy of history is the reason the cult of Ptah failed to strike permanent root in the Egyptian mind. According to Budge, the concept of a divine spirit, who created all by the power of his thought and the efficacy of his word, was too great and too simple for the popular mind to grasp.[5] The possibility of a mighty forward stride in the religious life of the nation was present at that early age, but it failed to materialize. The words of Paul well describe the great tragedy of pagan obscurantism: "They exchanged the truth about God for a lie and worshiped and served the creature rather than the Creator."[6]

After the Fourth Dynasty the priesthood of Heliopolis regained ascendancy, and Ra was promoted to the head of the pantheon as Re-Itum. Many kings of the Fifth Dynasty carried names compounded with Ra (Re) such as Sahure, Neferkare, and Neuserre. In the frame of the Heliopolitan cosmogony the pharaoh was considered as the incarnation of Horus and the son of Ra, these concepts finding expression in the first, third, and fifth names of the royal titulary. Though flattering to the ruler, the fiction of the divinity of the pharaoh seemed to have a stultifying effect on subsequent religious thought. In the first place, human dignity was bound to be diminished in sheer contrast to the glory of the "god on earth." If a nobleman had been allowed to kiss the foot of his majesty, instead of kissing the earth as the protocol required, that privilege was considered worthy of being engraved on his tomb. Unless redressed by the pharaoh it was considered a bad omen if the scepter of the sovereign accidentally touched any mortal.[7]

Many texts represent the pharaoh as ascending to heaven at death to join his father Ra in the solar bark. Immortality was his kingly prerogative. The most elaborate preparations were made to ensure the pharaoh's admission to life beyond, from the embalming of the body which took seventy days, to the erection of monumental tombs with attached funerary chapels where offerings were to be perpetually presented. The pyramid tombs may be conceived as stairways to heaven, just as the ziggurat towers of Mesopotamia.[8] The mystery of death, even in the case of the "divine" pharaoh, remained impenetrable and for that reason became a morbid concern. If death was a riddle to be overcome by sheer pomp and ritual, for the "divine" and "immortal" king, what hope was there for the hapless ordinary mortal?

Eventually the notion sprang into existence that the royal entourage of ladies and court officials might share immortality as attendants of their king, who might need their services in his afterlife. Thus the custom arose of building the mastaba tombs for members of the royal family and of the nobility along neatly traced streets close to the pyramid. And, most likely, all the commoners who had rendered service in the building of the pyramid with its complex of funeral temples entertained the hope that they, too, might share in the life to come. This might explain the willingness, perhaps eagerness, with which people of all walks of life engaged in the building of a royal pyramid.

There seemed to be no need of forced labor or even *corvée* work, for as long as the myth of the divinity of the kings lasted, the colossal task of erecting pyramids was a joint enterprise of nobles and commoners to ensure eternal life. Their common effort was, then, simply another variation on the theme, "salvation by works." And, of course, there were always a few among the skeptics and atheists who, as tomb-robbers, regarded the mortuary preparations as an opportunity for enriching themselves.

But the gearing of the total life of the nation to the thankless task of overcoming death eventually drained the resources of the country. No matter how rich the gold mines of Nubia or of the Wadi Hammamat, or how plentiful the harvests produced by the rich black soil annually flooded by the Nile, or how favorable the balance of trade with Byblos or Crete, the burying of the equivalent of millions of dollars in precious metals and mortuary furnishings at the death of every pharaoh (as may be judged by the wealth interred in the tomb of Tutankhamen) was bound to impoverish the country. Not only was wealth immobilized in tombs, but the endowments necessary to keep thousands of priests performing funerary rites in hundreds of shrines further depleted national resources.

The result of this single-hearted preoccupation with the dead is evident in the economic decay during the Sixth Dynasty, culminating in the total administrative chaos of the First Intermediate Period. First, pyramids decreased in size. Then they were made only of brick. Finally construction stopped altogether.

As the wealth of the pharaohs decreased, so did their prestige. Nobles were no longer eager to build their mastabas by the tombs of their sovereign, preferring to erect them in their own homes. In proportion to the dissipation of the myth of the divinity of the pharaoh, the unity of the "Two Lands" which "met in Memphis" weakened, until virtually the entire country reverted to a feudal state. The Manetho's legend of the seventy kings of the Seventh Dynasty who ruled seventy days is descriptive of the political anarchy that swept over the weakened country and lasted more than two centuries.

This time of trouble saw Egyptian life wrenched out of its traditional moorings and occasioned deep soul-searching. The "Lamentation of Ipuwer" reflects the bewilderment caused by the breakdown of the old order.[9] Aristocratic families which once basked in royal favor were reduced to poverty. *Nouveaus riches* flaunted their ill-gained wealth to the despair of the ancient aristocrats. "Behold, he who was buried as a falcon [now lies] on a [mere] bier. What the pyramid hid has become empty," reads the old dirge. Time-honored clichés were questioned. In a "Dialogue of a Man With His Soul," man weary of life contemplates suicide as the means of escaping to a happier existence. The document paints the attraction of death in glowing colors. Passing strange is the fact that in the dialogue the soul protests against the macabre idea by stating that it is better to enjoy this life, for no one is sure of the next. Yet in the Old Kingdom when the king was esteemed as the guarantor of the divine order in which every man found his happy niche, suicide had been unthinkable.

The downgrading of the concept of the divinity of the king was paralleled by a growing feeling of individual responsibility before God, which led to a greater emphasis on moral conduct. "The Instruction for King Meri-ka-Re"[10] made every man responsible before a divine judge for his conduct on earth. "Do justice whilst thou endurest upon earth. Quiet the weeper; do not oppress the widow; supplant no man in the property of his father," the old king advised. Farther on he made this sage observation: "More acceptable is the character of one upright of heart than the ox of the evildoer."

Driven out of their complacency by the collapse of the old order, men were obliged to rethink their status in the cosmos. The turmoil of the times acted as a fresh breeze upon man's dormant faculties, and one can only guess what the results might have been if the hoary hand of dead traditions had not paralyzed the incipient process of independent thought.

One new influence was the cult of Osiris, god of the dead, who gradually usurped the place of Ra and became his overlord. Moreover, his domain, originally restricted to the subterranean west, eventually encompassed the whole sky. Theological concepts changed from the writing of the Pyramid Texts to that of the Coffin Texts. The latter, written on the stone coffins or sarcophagi, repeat, elaborate, and expand much that is found in the Pyramid Texts. But whereas the Pyramid Texts gave right of entrance to heaven only to the king, the Coffin Texts, through the priests of Osiris, opened heaven to both noble and commoner.

The cult of Osiris with its idea of a final judgment might have helped effect a higher moral conduct for all society. But unhappily, because Osiris did not remain an ideal model, it did not elevate morals. On the contrary, the belief was fostered that any mortal might, through proper ritual and incantation, become as blameless as Osiris himself. According to a popular myth, Osiris had been murdered by Set and, even after his resurrection by the intervention of Isis and Horus, was again accused by Set before the gods. He convinced the judges of his innocence and was declared "true of voice," that is, "justified." By and by the appelative "true of voice" was appropriated for every mortal and in the long run came to mean little more than "deceased."[11]

It is lamentable that the noble principles expressed in the literature of the Herekleopolitan time were soon stifled by the dry formalism of the religion of Osiris. A few energetic minds might have grasped the

Horus. The living Pharaohs believed themselves incarnations of this falcon-headed god. Bronze sculpture in Louvre, Paris. Historical Pictures Service, Chicago.

idea that this world is a moral arena on which man stands before God as a responsible being. Man lingered for a moment on the threshold of a fresh advance in religious thought, but in the end he blindly turned away, and the idea was soon blurred by the surrounding darkness.

The bane of Egyptian religion was the widespread belief in magic. The Egyptian word for magic, *heka,* "made a god of its possessor superior in power to every being who did not possess it. By it alone a god was able to exist, and do the work which he did."[12] In the definition of Erman, "Magic is a barbarous offshoot of religion, and is an attempt to influence the powers that preside the destinies of mankind."[13] Whoever possessed *heka* was a magician, and through its efficacy he could coerce even the gods to perform his will.

The greatest of all magicians was Thoth, revered as the inventor of writing, the arts, and the sciences. It was he who taught the goddess Isis the spells whereby she restored Osiris to life after his murder by Set and expelled the poison from the body of her son Horus after he was stung by the scorpion sent by Set. He was likewise the god who healed the eye of Ra after it had been damaged and blinded by Set, restoring it to its original place in the face of Ra.

The Book of the Dead, copies of which were placed within the coffin, was an enlargement and commentary on the Coffin Texts intended to ensure the safe passage of the deceased into the netherworld. Hundreds of copies have survived, but as a rule even a "complete" scroll contains only part of the one hundred fifty or more known chapters.[14] Chapter 125 deals with the well-known judgment scene before Osiris. In the presence of Thoth who could read men's thoughts, the heart of the deceased was weighed against the feather of the goddess Ma'at, symbol of justice, or against the owner himself, as shown in one of the oldest scrolls, the *Theban Book of the Dead.* According to some manuscripts the judgment takes place in the presence of forty-two assessors which, as has been suggested, correspond to the local gods of the forty-two nomes or provinces. The deceased is supposed to mention the name of each assessor and deny a sin to each in turn. The complete list of sins, which shows much repetition and overlapping, is known as the Negative Confession. The first confession is "O thou of long strides, who makest thine appearance in Anna; I am not a doer of wrong"; the thirteenth reads, "O Eater of Blood, who makest thine appearance at the Block; I have not slaughtered the sacred animals."[15]

This raises an important question: Did the Egyptian regard moral excellence as a prerequisite to a share in the afterlife? Were his statements thought to be factual or magical? Faced with a *Book* composed for the most part of magic spells, one is inclined to believe that the Negative Confession, though revealing some uneasiness concerning sin, is magical in intent. A magical spell, if correctly uttered, was believed to bring to pass the very thing which was stated. The fourth section of chapter 125, known as the Rubric, confirms this assessment. In it "the reader is assured that if it be written 'upon a clean brick of clay, extracted from a field in which no swine hath trod, . . . he shall not be cut off at any gate of Amenta, but he shall be conveyed along with the kings of North and South, and make his appearance as a follower of Osiris: undeviatingly and for times infinite.' "[16]

Among the anxieties the *Book of the Dead* intended to allay, is that the deceased might forget his identity, or might not have a mouth with which to speak to the gods, or might be robbed of his heart, or that his head might be cut off, or his body, notwithstanding embalmment, might decay. For each one there was an appropriate magical formula to be uttered. Erman was undoubtedly right when he stated that once magic has taken root in the thinking of a nation, "there is no check on it, and by the side of the noble plant of religion there flourishes this fantastic weed of magic."[17]

The "times of trouble" of the First Intermediate Period had undermined the concept of the divinity of the pharaoh. In the Middle Kingdom he regained his lost prestige, but at the cost of showing concern for social justice and the well-being of the common people. Attention has been called to the careworn face of the pharaohs of this period as reflected in the statuary. The ancient zest for life and action, as illustrated in tomb scenes, is recovered, but balanced by a deeper moral concern. The greatness of a man is henceforth judged not by the size of his tomb, but by his deeds of righteousness, as the following quotation shows: "Be not evil: patience is good. Make thy memorial to last through the love of thee."[18] Frankfort maintains that this was an age of real social conscientiousness, in which "the psychological and moral basis was the belief that every man is the careworthy creation of the god."[19]

Another effect of the "time of trouble" had been the greater democratization of society, perceptible in the Coffin Texts. Whereas the Pyramid Texts, written upon the passages and chambers of the royal tomb, ensured only to the pharaoh a safe passage to the next world, the Coffin Texts were intended to benefit any mortal. This democratic trend is also attested by the fact that whereas in the Old Kingdom a common mortal was never represented in funerary reliefs in the act of worshiping a deity, this privilege being reserved to the monarch, from the Twelfth Dynasty on such representations became increasingly common.[20]

That all men were given equal opportunity by creation stands out in the following remarkable passage, from the Coffin Texts, quoted by Breasted:[21]

"I have made the four winds *that every man might breathe thereof like his brother* during his time.

"I have made the great waters that the *pauper like the lord* might have use of them.

"I have made *every man like his brother,* and I have forbidden that they do evil, (but) it was their hearts which undid that which I said."

This is the quaint Egyptian way of saying that all men were created equal, and that all had equal access to air and water, that is, equal opportunity to succeed. Any departure from this divine order is to be blamed on men, not the god. Along the same line, "The Eloquent Peasant" insists on the rights of the individual and the duty of the magistrate to uphold these rights.

The thought that the individual had value per se held immense possibilities for religious and moral growth. To recognize the individual as a responsible moral agent was in itself a significant forward stride in religious self-understanding. But the full impact of this concept was thwarted by the parallel development of superstition and magic. One practical effect of this equalitarian ideal was that any individual might rise in public office from the lowest position as scribe to the highest magistracy on sheer merit. Many tomb autobiographies tell of rapid promotions in the army or civil service because of the bravery or administrative talents of the individual. Rigid social stratification made its appearance only after the Twentieth Dynasty. There is no justification for retrojecting into the far past the caste system Herodotus noticed on his visit to Egypt in the middle of the fifth century B.C.

These and other qualities make the Middle Kingdom the high-water mark of Egyptian civilization. After three centuries of stable rule, Egypt entered another period of turmoil known to historians as the Second Intermediate Period. At the end of the Twelfth Dynasty divisive forces once more fractured the country, and competing dynasties ruled from Xois, Thebes, and possibly other centers. But the consequences of this second "time of troubles" were altogether different from the first.

The Hyksos invasion shattered the sense of security from external attacks born of sovereign past history and buttressed by geographical isolation. The harsh rule of the Hyksos, though brief (perhaps not more than a century), traumatized the Egyptian mind, engendering what Frankfort called "a psychosis of fear."[22] The collective effort to drive out the invader welded the nation as never before, but Egypt came out of this experience a totalitarian state.

Unprecedented regimentation grew at the expense of private initiative. It had not been enough to have driven the invaders from the delta. The hated Hyksos were to be crushed in their Asiatic home base. The war policy of Amose of the Eighteenth Dynasty was continued by Thutmose I, who crossed the Euphrates into the land of Mitanni.

The "psychosis of fear" was artificially promoted by the military class, avid for spoil and promotion, and eventually by the great priesthoods which became the chief beneficiaries of the Asiatic campaigns, as the victorious pharaohs brought their tribute to the gods. And the once modest temples of the Middle Kingdom began to grow through the benefactions of such kings as Thutmose III (who carried out sixteen campaigns in Asia), Seti I, and Ramses II, to mention only the most outstanding. The army was organized into four divisions and placed under the aegis of the gods Amon, Ra, Ptah, and Suthek, showing the close alliance of the army with the priesthood. The great Harris Papyrus, which lists the endowments of the different temples in the time of Ramses III, shows, according to the estimate of Schaedel, that by that time the temples owned one out of every five inhabitants of the nation and almost one third of the cultivable land. The lion's share belonged to the temple of Amon in Thebes, which, through its immense wealth, flexed powerful political muscles. The time came when the high priest of Amon in Thebes would finally claim the throne under Herihor of the Twenty-first Dynasty.

The brief interlude of the Amarna Age must be regarded, at least in part, as a protest against the overbearing ascendancy of the priesthood of Amon in Thebes. The fulcrum of this reaction was Amenhotep IV (Ikhnaton) (c. 1375 - c. 1366), whom historians have called the first *individual* in history. With him, the cult of Aton, barely incipient in the reign of his father, eclipsed that of all other gods. A syncretism of the sun-god Ra with Itum of Heliopolis, or Amon of Thebes, or with the god of the horizon under the appellation Re-Har-Akhti, was latent in Egyptian thought but had never issued into pure monotheism.

The implications of empire may have set in motion universalizing tendencies. After all, the same sun shed its blessings upon the countries in distant Asia to the east as on Lybia to the west. What may have been a vague intuition with others, with Amenophis IV became a fanatical conviction: Aton, the physical disk of the sun, source of all blessings, whose beneficent rays communicated life to all beings, was to be worshiped as the *only god*.

A chapel to sun-god Aton had been erected in Thebes under Amenhotep III, and an inscription is known of a certain Ra-mose who was both priest of Amon and "Steward in the Temple of Aton."[23] In the sixth year of his reign the young Amenhotep IV changed his name to Ikhnaton, "he who is beneficent to Aton," and embarked upon a wholesale campaign against the cult of Amon.

The old priesthood of Amon, whose vested interests were at stake, greeted the new king with sullen resistance, so much so that Ikhnaton removed the royal residence from Thebes to Akhetaton (modern Tell el-Amarna), a vast plain three hundred miles down the Nile.

Here, unhampered by entrenched conservatism, Ikhnaton gave free reign to his ideas in religion and art. A dogma of the new faith seems to have been fidelity to *ma'at,* "truth," which meant naturalism in art and candor in public life, including that of the royal court. Old artistic canons, like the law of frontality in statuary, must give place to the actual representation of what is seen. The idealized sculpture of the kings in serene detachment is substituted by realism, even if it meant representing the pharaoh with his elongated head and protruding abdomen. On the other hand, the new art could produce such masterpieces as the bust of Queen Nefertiti, or the exquisite painting of natural scenery, as, for example, a cat prowling through the reeds in a marsh.

The noblest expression of the religious thought of the Amarna Age is unquestionably the often quoted hymn to Aton which in touching terms describes the divine care for all creation. Carved on the wall of the tomb of the courtier Eye, who is depicted in a praying position with his wife, it is believed by many to have been composed by Ikhnaton himself. The parallels it shows with Psalm 104 are to be explained by the common theme as was then universally felt rather than to actual borrowing in one direction or the other.

If Ikhnaton had entertained any hope that great numbers of Egyptians would adopt the new religion, he was bound to disappointment. The average Egyptian was an eclectic by temperament and sensed no contradiction between the differing theologies of Memphis and Heliopolis; rather he vaguely regarded them all as complementary explanations of the ultimate reality. And Ikhnaton's insistence on a single sweeping generalization to explain the many-sided aspects of nature, no matter how convincing, served finally to offend age-old prejudices.

One glaring weakness of the new faith was the position occupied by Ikhnaton himself. While he and his immediate family might claim single-hearted devotion to Aton, his courtiers and the populace in the new capital were taught to look to Ikhnaton himself as the bestower of temporal and eternal benefits. He was referred to as "the good god." Prayers were offered to him. Tomb scenes show him worshiping Aton the "living" sun disk, but all the courtiers are bowing in adoration of Ikhnaton himself, the god-king. Wilson sums up the situation as follows: "The self-centered nature of Akh-en-Aton's [Ikhnaton's] faith, the fact that only the royal family had a trained and reasoned loyalty to the Aton, and the fact that all of pharaoh's adherents were forced to give their entire devotion to him as god-king explain why the new religion collapsed after Akh-en-Aton's death."[24] In sum, the person of the king played such an overly central role in Atonism that it could not serve as an enduring vehicle to pure monotheistic faith.

There was, in addition, a marked lack of ethics in the religion of Aton. The stress on *ma'at* "truth" seemed to imply no more than candor and openness. "The old is wrong, and the new is right"; but there is no call to purity of motives or to righteousness of conduct. Herein lies the sharpest contrast between Atonism and Hebrew monotheism, which insisted upon upright ethical behavior.

Soon after the death of Ikhnaton Egypt repudiated the Aton "heresy" wholesale. Under his successor Tutankhamen the new capital was abandoned, Thebes became once more the religious and political center, and the god Amon was restored to royal favor. Just as under Ikhnaton's rule the name Amon had been expunged from untold inscriptions, it was now the fate of Aton to have his name hacked from the temples and monuments and to be relegated to oblivion in the restored pantheon.

The Amarna interlude had lasted only a decade, but it would be rash to conclude that its influence ceased with that one blow. Its effects continued to be felt in greater naturalism in art and in the elevation of colloquial speech to the official language of the New Kingdom. Nor was the monotheism latent in Egyptian thought completely obliterated.

A papyrus from the Nineteenth Dynasty treats Amon as the summation of all other important gods. We quote a short excerpt: "All gods are three: Amon, Re [Ra], and Ptah, and there is no second to them. 'Hidden' is his name as Amon, he is Re in face, and his body is Ptah. . . . Only he is: Amon, with Re, [and with Ptah]—together three."[25]

In another set of hymns (dating from the late Nineteenth Dynasty) Amon appears as a universal god, who assumes the functional roles of other gods and is regarded as the creator of all, "who spoke with his mouth and there came into existence all men, gods, large and small cattle in their entirety, and all that which flies and lights."[26] Yet these flashes of religious insight were isolated and had little effect upon popular religion with its increasing devotion to the cult of Osiris, the ruler of the dead.

Tomb stelae from a workmen's cemetery some time after the Amarna Age reveal yet a new ethos. In these inscriptions the humility of the worshiper contrasts "with the self-assured tone and the assumption of infallibility pervading all the earlier religious literature."[27] In one inscription Amon is entreated as "that beloved God who hearkens to humble entreaties, who stretches forth his hand to the humble, who saves the weak, . . . who hears prayers, comes at the voice of the distressed humble one, who gives breath to him that is wretched."

A slightly later age reflected the same stress on quietude, humility, and personal piety, as is shown by "The Instruction of Ani." Remarkable among these bits of counsel is the following: "Do not talk a lot. Be silent, and thou wilt be happy. Do not be garrulous. The dwelling of god, its abomination is clamor. Pray thou with a loving heart, all the words of which are hidden, and he will do what thou needest, he will hear what thou sayest, and he will accept thy offering."[28] No god's name is mentioned, the deity being referred to merely as "thy god" or "the god." This reticence may well be due to an unspoken feeling that over and above the gods there is one supreme god whose name is ineffable.

A similar restraint observable in "The Instruction of Amen-em-Opet," of a much later date, possibly from the seventh to the sixth centuries, may be explained by its secular nature. Only three gods are mentioned, Min, Horus, and Thoth, and these only incidentally. According to R. Anthes, this book differs from older Egyptian wisdom books by its humbler and less materialistic outlook. On the other hand it narrowed the scope of man's self-determination by its stress on the god Fate and the goddess Fortune in whose hands lay the destiny of man. This fatalistic outlook on life, though encouraging personal piety on one side, also promoted a greater reliance upon the rites and magical practice inherited from the past.

By the end of the New Empire, Egypt had outlived her period of spiritual creativity. The last millennium of her political life was characterized by external weakness and internal stagnation. Flattering herself with past achievements, she ceased to grope for truth. J. A. Wilson expresses his belief that "the very qualities which suggest the claim that Egypt was highly civilized suggest also that she lacked self-criticism, that she never achieved profundity, and she never felt the burning inner urge to achieve new and daring conquests of mind and spirit. . . . Egypt's strength was such that she did not feel the need for renewed strength until it was too late."[29]

During the short periods of national revival under the Saite Dynasty, or under the Nectanebos of the Thirtieth Dynasty, the best

Egypt could do was to indulge in archaizing art and religion without the ability to infuse new life into old forms. Egyptian religion had become as lifeless as a mummy. Nonetheless, as a mummy shrouded in a veil of mystery, it awed pagan Greece and Rome and even found a shrine within the walls of the city on the Tiber.

Egypt's allotted period of grace finally ran out. She had failed in her search after the true God, even though "He is not far from each one of us."[30] In man's quest for ultimate truth, the wisdom of the Egyptians proved in the end to be a blind guide.

NOTES AND REFERENCES

1. Acts 17:27.
2. E. A. Wallis Budge, *From Fetish to God in Ancient Egypt,* page vi. See also pages 16 and 139.
3. J. B. Pritchard, ed., *Ancient Near East Texts,* second edition, page 5.
4. See Budge, *op. cit.,* pp. 146, 147.
5. *Ibid.,* p. 270.
6. Romans 1:25.
7. On the awe-inspiring majesty that surrounded the pharaoh, see H. A. Frankfort comments in *The Intellectual Adventure of Ancient Man,* page 75.
8. For a recent study of the function of the pyramid, see Alexander Badawy, "The Ideology of the Superstructure of the Mastaba Tomb in Egypt," *Journal of Near Eastern Studies,* Vol. 15 (1956), pp. 180-183.
9. Pritchard, *op. cit.,* pp. 441 ff.
10. *Ibid.,* pp. 414 ff.
11. The exact meaning of *m3' ḫru* has been discussed by different scholars, and more recently by Rudolf Anthes, "The Original Meaning of *M3' Ḫru,*" *Journal of Near Eastern Studies,* Vol. 13 (1954), pp. 21 ff.
12. Wallis Budge, *op. cit.,* p. 116.
13. Erman, *Egyptian Religion,* London, 1907, p. 149 quoted by Wallis Budge, *op. cit.,* p. 114.
14. F. W. Read, *Egyptian Religion and Ethics,* page 98. Naville's edition of 1886 is based on a comparison of various manuscripts of the Eighteenth, Nineteenth, and Twentieth Dynasties, while retaining the chapter numbering of Lepsius whose translation was based on the great Turin Papyrus of Anf-ankh. The *Book* is abundantly illustrated with vignettes, the quality of which vary from copy to copy according to the resources of the owner. Little light is gained from its copious verbiage on Egyptian religious thought, for most chapters are made up of prayers, spells, and incantations to enable the deceased to overcome the numerous obstacles on the way to the abode of the blessed. Read calls it a "magical *vade mecum* for the future life."
15. *Ibid.,* p. 110.
16. *Ibid.,* p. 113.
17. Adolf Erman, *Egyptian Religion,* page 148. G. Steindorff disagrees in part with our conclusions. He asserts, "But it would be putting an undeserved slight upon the ethical ideas of the ancient Egyptians if we were to suppose that the destinies of man after death were regarded by them as solely dependent upon the knowledge and the recitation of the various magic formulae."—*The Religion of the Ancient Egyptians,* page 131.
18. "Teachings of Merikare," J. B. Pritchard, *op. cit.,* p. 415.

19. H. A. Frankfort in *Intellectual Adventure of Ancient Man,* page 109.
20. Jaroslav Černy, *Ancient Egyptian Religion,* page 67.
21. James H. Breasted, *The Dawn of Conscience,* page 221.
22. H. A. Frankfort, *op. cit.,* pp. 110, 111.
23. John A. Wilson, *The Culture of Ancient Egypt,* page 210.
24. *Ibid.,* p. 224.
25. *Ibid.,* p. 228.
26. *Ibid.,* p. 229.
27. Jaroslav Černy, *op. cit.,* p. 68.
28. J. B. Pritchard, *op. cit.,* p. 420.
29. John A. Wilson, *op. cit.,* pp. 145, 146.
30. Acts 17:27.

Chapter 7

Mesopotamian Civilization on Trial

The erection of the first city was recorded in Genesis[1] with deliberate intention. It meant, first of all, that man felt greater security in association with his fellows than in isolation. But association implied partial loss of personal freedom—a loss which could only increase with the complexity of this association. Notwithstanding, men in ever greater numbers decided that added security was worth the price of autonomy.

Corporate life would provide an imagined security because it relieved man of the burden of personal responsibility.[2] The effort to make moral decisions is painful. Most people preferred to eschew them or reduce them to a minimum. Man would try to share his moral responsibility with the group rather than face it individually. He would delegate his moral decisions and responsibilities to a leader rather than face the Judge of all the earth alone.

Man would cling to freedom—if it did not involve responsibility. But in a moral universe not of his own creation, he could not enjoy one and decline the other. Freedom and responsibility are both of one piece, like the two faces of the same coin. Man had been created free, yet was accountable to his Maker. For the sinner, accountability took the zest out of freedom, thus tipping the scale in favor of security.

Corporate life, then, became a convenient shield behind which to hide. There was security in anonymity, or so man thought. Man's consequent depersonalization contrasted startlingly with his pristine self-assertion. However, it was not the self-effacement of humility, but that of fear. Let the clan make the decisions for him. Let the city assume responsibility for his well-being. Let the state define for him his role in life. Man, who started out to shape his own destiny in defiance of God, was now willing to place his temporal and eternal destiny in the hands of the group. The path from freedom to enslavement was astonishingly rapid. To escape the loving hands of God, man was willing to place his freedom in the hands of sinners like himself.

The classic illustration of this drive for collective security is the building of the Tower of Babel. The gist of the narrative is humanity's urge for security. Subdued by the cataclysmic effects of the Flood and doubtful about the divine promise to Noah that no other flood would again "destroy all flesh,"[3] man attempted to work out his own salvation. Whereas God had planned salvation by His own promise to be accepted by faith, man in his defiant, alienated predicament devised a plan of salvation by works. This antithesis would persist throughout the ages and become the undergirding of all pagan religions. In the building of the tower converged the three basic drives of ancient man: the desire for collective security in the face of nature's threats, the urge to attain salvation by works rather than faith, and obstinate, blind pride ("let us make a name for ourselves").[4]

Collective security became a dynamic driving force behind all sociopolitical institutions. Clans, city-states, kingdoms, and finally empires all contained elements of this fearful drive for security. Evergrowing regimentation was the price paid for this real or imagined boon.

The subservience of the individual to the interests of the group is nowhere clearer than in the city-states of Sumer. Here the individual became an insignificant cog in the economic machinery regulated by the priests. Under the Akkadian empire the control shifted to the palace, but private initiative was just as effectively smothered under the royal bureaucracy. Whereas a benevolent ruler such as Urukagina of Lagash might work for the "common good," a power-drunk monarch such as Naram-Sin of Akkad regimented the populace into a military machine for his personal glory. Pride, the hunger for self-glorification, was cleverly superimposed on the urge for security to produce the convenient notion of kingship by divine right. This notion of divine kingship stands out clear in the preamble to the "Sumerian King List": "When kingship was lowered from heaven, kingship was first in Eridu."[5]

A jerry-built empire such as that of Sargon of Akkad, erected on the martial prowess of a single family, could not long endure. The clash of regional interests and a growing differentiation of cultures, as well as the greed for power by petty kings, collapsed the whole structure. Its geographic extent met no particular need at the time. The Guti, barbarians from Luristan, poured from the mountains, taking advantage of the weakness resulting from internal rivalries, illustrating how a hardier race, not yet softened by the effects of over regimentation, could defeat the "civilized" peoples of the Mesopotamian plains. During the century of Gutian control the conquerors absorbed the secure-rather-than-free temper of the conquered. What Capua did to the soldiers of Hannibal, Mesopotamian civilization did to the Guti. In two or three generations their moral fiber degenerated to the low level of the peoples they had subdued, and at last Utukhegal of Erech easily drove them back into their mountains.

Later the kingdom of Sumer and Akkad again broke up into rival city-states which, one by one, fell easy prey to a new wave of Semites breaking in from the Arabian desert, the Amorites. These nomads were, first of all, lovers of freedom. Thrown upon their own in the vast expanses of the desert, they developed strong individualists. They sought survival in the wastelands of Arabia, not within the mothering walls of a city, but within the resources of individual initiative and acumen. When they associated into clans by ties of blood, the sheik was invariably *primus inter pares,* first among peers, owing his ascendancy more to superior moral and mental qualities than to hereditary rights.

The nomads living on the fringe of the desert succumbed first to the lure of easier life on "the sown" areas. At first they contented themselves with raids on the cultivated territories adjacent to the Euphrates. Their richer neighbors retaliated, but the elusive nomads' familiarity with the desert compensated for their inferior numbers and weapons. A stalemate was eventually reached and the Amorites were allowed to settle on the marginal lands where their herds of sheep and goats could thrive. Almost imperceptibly the penetration proceeded. Sedentary life appealed to ever greater numbers, and within a few generations they felt at home in Mari, Babylon, Larsa, and Isin. Unspoiled by the pampered langor of civilization, they wrested control from their more sophisticated but less energetic Akkadian or Sumerian rulers in one city after another.

With Hammurabi the rulers of this dynasty give up Akkadian names. It is not mere coincidence that in the tension between two socioeconomic systems—the pastoral economy of the early Amorites with their stress upon individual freedom, and the agricultural and commercial economy of traditional Mesopotamia with the emphasis on interdependence—the need was felt for a new law code. Hammurabi tried to harmonize the two tendencies in his justly famous code of laws. Couched in casuistic style, stemming from the decisions of the courts of elders which had functioned from immemorial times, the provisions of the code give expression both to individual responsibility and to the penalties attached to different crimes.[6] In a milieu where individual rights were all but immersed in the rights of the crown and of the temple, Hammurabi's enlightened views effected a decided gain for individual freedom. Despotic governments refuse to state clearly the rules of the political game. By contrast the advancing march of freedom has invariably been bound with declarations of rights.

It may be an exaggeration to call the code of Hammurabi a declaration of rights, but in an age and place where the individual counted for so little, it amounted to that. All subsequent Mesopotamian periods look back to his as the golden age. The reason is obvious. In his age freedom was breaking through the mist of social and economic despotism that had smothered Mesopotamia for so long.

But true freedom could not coexist with the polytheistic religious conceptions of the day. Polytheism was inherently contradictory and anarchical. It fostered the notion of blind fate and despotism. In the Gilgamesh Epic, for example, the Flood was brought about by the irrational passion of Enlil. In the myth of "Adapa and the South Wind," Adapa forfeited eternal life through the blunder of Ea, who played the role of benefactor of humanity in the Gilgamesh Epic.[7] Polytheism was shot through with irrationality. Nature and man were subject to the unpredictable whims of the gods. Since no law was discernible in the realm of the gods, the notion of freedom under law could scarcely be entertained in the realm of man. The trend toward despotism and the stifling of the human spirit was inevitable.

The shaping of society in the form of a cosmic analogue might satisfy men as long as the realm of the gods presented a semblance of order. But man's search for meaning in the universe, as reflected in ever more complicated myths, at last reaches an impasse when no longer is any pattern or order discernible.

Oppenheim evaluates the decline of private economic enterprise during the following millennium of Mesopotamian history in the following words: "Such are the increased economic role of the palace organization, the decreasing influence of royal authority, the disappearance of private economic initiative and of all vestiges of social reforms—or experiments—that characterize the Hammurapi period. . . . The scarcity of legal documents related to private commercial activities (such as the buying and selling of real estate) or the making of wills and marriage settlements, the absence of documents referring to the hiring of persons and services, and the making of loans—so plentiful in earlier times—emphasize the decline of private initiative."[8] The same judgment could be passed on other phases of Mesopotamian life. Stagnation or paralysis best describes it, creeping over man's spirit whenever his existence becomes a meaningless puzzle.

Pari passu or concurrent with polytheism, demonism spread its bane over Babylonian society. Life in the squalid Mesopotamian cities was riddled with the fear of demons who beset ordinary mortals at every step. The state religion with its perfunctory ritual offered little to rid the common man of his dread of evil spirits. The great gods Enlil, Ea, and Marduk might concern themselves with the welfare of the nation and the king, but they forgot the individual citizen. The public played little or no part in the daily services of the great temples. At best the worshiper might catch a glimpse of the god carried in procession through the streets in festal celebrations, such as the Akitu festival every New Year. For comfort in his personal life he turned to his household gods revered within the family circle, or he might visit the chapel of a minor deity by the wayside. One such shrine has been identified in Ur through inscriptions. It is dedicated to the goddess Hendursanga believed to protect wanderers through the wilderness. Her devotees expressed their gratitude by depositing their offerings in the vestibule of the chapel.

Popular superstition populated the air with demons ever ready to trap mankind by their wiles. Abundant tablets containing spells to avert the "evil eye," or the incantations of witchcraft, known as the *Maklu* and *Shurpu* texts, testify to the widespread, soul-depressing belief in evil spirits.

The demise of Amorite ascendancy in Mesopotamia can be attributed to military defeat in the face of superior foes and to a certain amount of economic depression as the channels of commerce were blocked by the rising Hittites to the north and the Sea-land Dynasty to the south. Yet the Amorites suffered a spiritual death which lay behind their physical demise. Their "allotted period," to borrow a phrase from Paul's discourse in the Areopagus, ran out. The nation's opportunity for spiritual advancement, after a brief promise in Hammurabi's day, passed by almost unnoticed. Another racial group would have its day of grace on the Mesopotamian stage; God gave the next half millennium to the Kassites.

It was given in a most unexpected way. Through a twist of events historians are prone to call "accidents," king Hittite Murshulish I, flushed with recent victories in Syria, thunderbolted from the far north and raided Babylon about 1531 B.C. It might have been utopian for Murshulish to hold on to such a prize so distant from his home base in Asia Minor. But, bloated with plunder, the Hittite king turned about, leaving Babylon to its own fate. Seeing their opportunity, the Kassites, who for decades had been streaming southward from the Zagros Mountains, mastered the city of Babylon and part of Babylonia.

In the shifting political scene, as far as historians have been able to deduce from the meager inscriptions of the period, none of the Kassite rulers[9] made any great mark. Besides incorporating the Sea-land to the south under Ulamburiash, and resisting Assyrian encroachment from the north, the Kassites seemed to cherish no further territorial ambitions.

Some progress, though feeble, was made away from the degraded gods toward a more ethical religion by the Kassites. As seen on the *kudurru* or boundary stones of the period, the Kassites habitually represented their gods by abstract signs.[10] Moortgat relates[11] this lack of desire to humanize their gods to a general heightening of religious ethos and a greater stress upon moral content in religion. Apparently the "times of trouble" brought upon Babylon by the Kassite rule had thrust upon the native conscience the inevitable question: Why had the gods forsaken the land? Or, why had the land incurred their wrath? A recognition that sin had alienated the gods may have imposed itself. Based on this recognition, the Kassites may have concluded that divine protection may not be enjoyed without corresponding worthy moral conduct on the part of the people.

It had not been enough to go through the forms of an elaborate ritual to please the deity. If the nation persisted in breaking the principles of the moral order, the stately pomp of temple ritual was a mockery. A sharpened consciousness of sin seems to have resulted, with the concomitant notion that sin must be punished. The Kassites knew sin involved more than failure to comply with prescribed ritual. They recognized guilt as well in failure to measure up to the demands of justice in human relations, demands such as honesty, faithfulness to friends, and humane treatment of prisoners. Lambert finds an incipient awareness of guilt as early as the First Dynasty.[12]

And if sin brings down punishment, then righteousness would automatically ensure exemption from suffering. This in turn might easily be corrupted into a utilitarian or even legalistic motivation for good conduct. The flourishing wisdom literature of the period, which purported to furnish practical guidance to a good life, reflected this concept, as can be seen in the "Instructions of Shuruppak," "Counsels of Wisdom," "Counsels of a Pessimist," and the "Advice to a Prince." "Counsels of Wisdom" deals with such topics as avoidance of bad companions, improper speech, avoidance of altercations, kindness to those in need, and the duties and benefits of religion, all of which find close parallels in the Biblical book of Proverbs.

Unfortunately for the system, however, the facts of actual life did not fit easily into this moral straightjacket. It was not always self-evident that sin was followed by punishment or that a righteous life ensured bliss. Two long works of literature deal with this problem. One is the "Poem of the Righteous Sufferer," also known as "The Babylonian Job," or better yet by its first line, "I will praise the lord of wisdom." Lambert dates this poem in the Kassite period.[13] The poem's main point is the sufferer's complaint about the inscrutability of the gods. In the following lines this theme stands out in particular:

I wish I knew that these things were pleasing to one's god!
What is proper to oneself is an offense to one's god,
What in one's own heart seems despicable is proper to one's god.
Who knows the will of the gods in heaven?
Who understands the plans of the underworld gods?
Where have mortals learnt the way of a god?[14]

The "Babylonian Theodicy," an acrostic poem of twenty-seven stanzas with eleven lines each, written shortly after the Kassite period,[15] presents an argument between two friends, one complaining that he is suffering through no fault of his own, the other trying to justify the ways of god. The sufferer's friend makes the following points: (1) that suffering is the common lot of mankind, (2) that a life of piety will not go unrewarded, (3) that the divine mind is inscrutable, (4) that in the end the sinner is brought low, and (5) that the gods made men prone to injustice. This disconcerting conclusion is brought out in lines 279 and 280:

[The gods] gave perverse speech to the human race.
With lies, and not truth, they endowed them forever.[16]

If the "friends" of the Biblical Job erred by blaming Job himself for his sufferings, *this* sufferer's "friend" blundered more seriously by blaming the *deity* for man's sin. In this poem there is a glimpse of neither the vicarious nor the disciplinary value of suffering. The fatalistic ideas of the Bablyonians blighted religious insight, blunted the sense of sin and guilt, and denied individual responsibility.

The appraisal of H. Frankfort is telling. "The Mesopotamians, while they knew themselves to be subject to the decrees of the gods, had no reason to believe that these decrees were necessarily just. Hence their penitential psalms abound in confessions of guilt but ignore the sense of sin; they are vibrant with despair but not with contrition—with regret but not with repentance. The Mesopotamian recognized guilt by its consequences: when he suffered, he assumed that he had transgressed a divine decree. . . .

"Thus everything pertaining to human guilt was likely to assume a mechanistic and gloomy aspect. For a chosen people conformance with the will of God can be a source of joy. For the Mesopotamians the divine decrees merely circumscribed man's servitude."[17]

Since his fate was thought to be in the hands of such gods, man

Nebuchadnezzar. Despite his seven-year bout with insanity, this powerful king built up Babylon to a pinnacle of glory during his forty-three-year reign. Fanciful representation by William Blake in Tate Gallery, London. Historical Pictures Service, Chicago.

was not considered free to act responsibly. This negation of freedom paved the way for the pernicious doctrine of fatalism which permeated Babylonian religion more and more until, with its sense of sin and guilt blunted, the civilization it formed was finally extinguished.

Once again foreign invaders, this time the Elamites, raided Babylon (c. 1155 B.C.) and, without occupying the land, paved the way for the downfall of the Kassite dynasty. The national Babylonian party placed one of their own on the throne, thus inaugurating the Second Dynasty of Isin.[18]

No doubt there were political and military reasons for the debacle of the Kassites. They were never more than a leading minority. They may have lost their right to leadership by lack of nerve and competence. Judging from their religious literature, they had sunk into a fatalistic *laissez-faire* which provided no stimulus to moral responsibility. And with no further contribution to make either culturally or morally, they failed as had those earlier peoples.

The next half millennium of Babylonian history is characterized by the efforts of two new closely related racial groups to gain political ascendancy in Mesopotamia, namely, the Arameans and the Chaldeans. Their efforts were frustrated first by the resistance of the native rulers of Isin and later by the growing might of Assyria. After the short-lived success of Marduk-apal-idin (Biblical Merodach-baladan) in the days of Sargon II of Assyria and his successor, the Chaldeans, following on the wake of the decline of Assyria, made a second bid for power under Nabopolassar (626 B.C.), and this time obtained control. The Chaldeans, aided by the Medes, destroyed Ninevah in 612 B.C. For nearly a century, particularly during the brilliant reign of Nebuchadnezzar who restored the city to its ancient glory, Babylon experienced a second renaissance.

For all its splendor, this Babylonian revival was anticlimactic. The heavy hand of the religiopolitical establishment soon stifled the Chaldean drive for power. With the exception of Nabopolassar and his son Nebuchadnezzar, the rulers of this dynasty lacked administrative talent and military prowess. Institutionalized religion resisted change. The past was normative. Nebuchadnezzar and, even more, Nabonidus looked nostalgically to the achievements of a Naram-Sin or Ur-Nammu and tried to recapture some of the pristine glory. Old temples were identified and repaired. Nabonidus, for example, reports how he discovered an inscription of Ur-Nammu and his son Shulgi in Ur, from which he concluded that the ziggurat which Ur-Nammu had begun to build was finished by his son, adding that he repaired the ziggurat with mortar and burned brick. In a similar vein he tells how he rebuilt the temple of Shamash in Larsa founded by Barnaburiash.[19]

Nabonidus was trying to revive the hoary ruins of a civilization that for all practical purposes was dead. To inject new life into the body was beyond his ability. Patch-up was all he achieved. Not even the incantations of wizards and soothsayers could perform the miracle. Isaiah confronted Babylon with the irony: "Stand fast in your enchantments and your many sorceries, with which you have labored from your youth; perhaps you may be able to succeed, perhaps you may inspire terror. You are wearied with your many counsels; let them stand forth and save you, those who divide the heavens, who gaze at the stars, who at the new moon predict what shall befall you."[20]

Here Isaiah mocks at what was one of the last and most popular developments in Babylonian religion. Stargazing had been an ancient pastime of priests, but only in the two centuries before the fall of Babylon did astrology obtain status.[21] Associating the leading gods with the planets, the Babylonians thought they could read their will in the sky. The day finally came when no significant public or private decision was taken without consulting an astrologer.

The superstition of astrology provided another convenient escape from individual responsibility. Since the stars determine fate, no one is blamed for his failures. Indeed the dead weight of fatalism would further smother whatever residue of the sense of freedom and responsibility man might still possess. Polytheism with its inner moral contradictions, demonism with the paralyzing dread it inspired, sorcery with its superstitious pretense of manipulating the higher powers to one's ends, and now fatalism with its newfangled astrological garb competed to destroy human dignity and responsibility.

The prophet underscored inordinate pride as another reason for Babylon's fall.[22] The theme that inordinate pride must be followed by divine punishment, that *hubris* is punished by *nemesis,* which stands out so clearly in Greek popular thought, appears over and again in the pages of the Bible: "Pride goes before destruction, and a haughty spirit before a fall." "Whoever exalts himself will be humbled."[23] The prophet indicts Babylon in a similar vein: "You said in your heart, 'I am, and there is no one besides me.' But evil shall come upon you, for which you cannot atone."[24] From Nebuchadnezzar we have statements such as this: "In Babylon, the city which I prefer, which I love, was the palace, the amazement of the people, the bond of the land, the brilliant palace, the abode of majesty on the ground of Babylon."[25] Or the song:

> O Babylon, whosoever beholds thee is filled with rejoicing,
> Whosoever dwells in Babylon increases his life,
> Whosoever speaks evil of Babylon is like one who kills his own mother,
> Babylon is like a sweet date palm, whose fruit is lovely to behold.[26]

The prophet's indictment is directed not against any king in particular, but against the city and empire. Babylonians regarded their city as the "navel" of the world, or "the origin and center of all lands." Undoubtedly the sanctuary of Marduk, the chief of all the gods, standing in the city, conferred upon it exceptional prestige. The dazzling temple-complex of *Esagila* with its tower *Etemenanki* was one of the wonders of the world. Such pride engendered a false sense of security which in turn fanned the flames of still greater pride. Whether overtly expressed or not, Babylon felt secure in her accomplishments and prestige. She had attained, so she thought, that for which generations had been groping—total security. Astrology gave her the key to the secrets of the gods. Even the future was no longer an impenetrable mystery. But the moment inordinate pride found expression in the arrogant claim—"Is not this great Babylon, which I have built by my mighty power . . . for the glory of my majesty?"[27]—divine decree ordered its nemesis.

NOTES AND REFERENCES

1. Genesis 4:17-22.

2. On corporate personality see Wheeler Robinson, *The People and the Book,* ed. A. S. Peake, 1925, pp. 276ff., J. Pedersen, *Israel: Its Life and Culture* I-II, 1926, pp. 271 ff., A. R. Johnson, *The One and the Many,* 1942.

3. Genesis 9:15.

4. J. B. Pritchard, ed., *Ancient Near Eastern Texts,* p. 265.

5. A. Moortgat, *Geschichte Vorderasiens bis zum Hellenismus* (München: Verlag F. Bruckmann, 1959), page 273.

6. E. A. Speiser, discussing the code of Hammurabi, wrote: "In essence, *mesarum*

(justice) is the process whereby law is made to function equitably. This is one of the ruler's principal duties. It involves supervision, adjustment, amendments. An able administrator may find it necessary to make the up-to-date compilations of normative provisions. Hammurabi did that, and so before him did Lipitishtar and Bilalama, Ur-Nammu and apparently also Urukagina. The ruler who has fulfilled these obligations, or claims to have done so, is described as *sar mesarim* 'the just king.' "—"Authority and Law in Mesopotamia" in *Authority and Law in the Ancient Orient* (Supplement to the *Journal of the American Oriental Society,* N. 17, 1954), page 12.

7. For a detailed analysis of the Adapa myth see Erich Voegelin, *Order and History,* I, pages 18 ff.

8. A. Leo Oppenheim, *Ancient Mesopotamia,* page 159.

9. From the names of their gods, such as Maruttash or Buriash (= Greek Boreas), as well as from the few remnants of their language, it is believed that the Kassites had been in contact with Indo-European tribes, or even led by Aryans.

10. See S. J. Schwantes, *A Short History of the Ancient Near East,* page 42.

11. See *Agypten und Vorderasien im Altertum,* page 335.

12. W. G. Lambert finds an incipient awareness of guilt as early as the First Dynasty of Babylon. See his book *Babylonian Wisdom Literature,* pages 10 ff.

13. *Ibid.,* p. 15.

14. *Ibid.,* p. 41.

15. W. G. Lambert dates the poem from about 1000 B.C.

16. *Ibid.,* pp. 65, 66.

17. *Kingship and the Gods,* pages 278, 279.

18. Hartmut Sehmökel, *Geschichte des Alten Vorderasien,* page 181.

19. See H. Frankfort, *op. cit.,* p. 268.

20. Isaiah 47:12, 13.

21. Centuries of observation had led to the conclusion that the planets, only five of which were known, meandered through the firmament of stars. Since the stars kept their relative positions constant, constellations were identified until the whole sky was mapped. Due to its fixed position the polar star was recognized, and those forming a band around the celestial equator were divided into twelve zones covering thirty degrees each. The zones of the zodiac were named by the constellations they comprised, most of which carried an animal name, of which the word zodiac is a reminder. Eventually each month was associated with a zodiac sign, which was thought to determine the fate of the individual born under it. In addition certain conjunctions of the planets with the zones of the zodiac were interpreted as signs of good or bad omen.

22. See Isaiah 47:7, 8, 10, 11. See A. Toynbee, *A Study of History* abrgd. by D. C. Somervell, pages 308, 309.

23. Proverbs 16:18; Matthew 23:12.

24. Isaiah 47:10, 11.

25. E. Schrader, *Keilinschriftlich Bibliothek,* Vol. 3, part 2, p. 25.

26. E. Ebeling, *Keilschrifttexte aus Assur religiösen Inhalts,* part 1, No. 8.

Of interest in this connection is the fact that with few exceptions, such as Naram-Sin of Akkad and Ibi-Sin of the Third Dynasty of Ur, Mesopotamian kings claimed no divine titles. On the other hand Assyrian kings in their inscriptions mince no words in their self-apotheosis, and quite likely this would prove to be the case of Babylonian kings if more documents were available. Since many such inscriptions were not intended for public reading, *e.g.,* foundation stones and tablets embedded in walls, but apparently were addressed to the gods, there is little justification for this pompous juxtaposition of titles. (A. Leo Oppenheim, *op. cit.,* pp. 144 ff.) That a simple mortal should try to awe his subjects with an array of boastful titles is admissible; but if the object was to impress the gods it was nothing short of blasphemous.

27. Daniel 4:30.

Chapter 8

A Prophet in Persia

"Thus says the Lord to His anointed, to Cyrus, whose right hand I have grasped, to subdue nations before him."[1] This note of goodwill toward Cyrus of Persia goes beyond the fact that he would exercise his influence for the rebuilding of Jerusalem and its temple. As the only foreign king to be called the Lord's "anointed," he would indeed set the Jewish exiles free from the Babylonian captivity. But over and above this immediate task, he would in some ulterior sense fulfill all of God's purpose.[2]

Cyrus's conquest of Babylon interrupted for a thousand years Semitic dominance in the Near East. Not until the Moslem conquests of the seventh century of our era would Semites again hold the banner of leadership there. But if the Syriac society had a second lease on life under the aegis of the Islamic faith, the old gods of Babylon, which held sway over man's mind for so long, had, with the permanent obliteration of their ancient temples in Ur, Nippur, Sippar, and other centers, crumbled forever in the dust.

A religion propped up by a political order such as that of Mesopotamia was bound to collapse when the sustaining political structure which lent it credibility no longer existed. As Voegelin points out, if Babylonian society was structured on the basis of a cosmic analogue, reciprocally, the political organization influenced their later concept of the cosmic order, as when, in the Babylonian revision of the Epic of Creation, Marduk replaces Enlil as the hero who establishes the present world order. And in a later Assyrian version of the epic, Ashur in turn replaces Marduk.[3]

Cyrus's sweeping victories over Media, Lydia, and Babylon, which allowed him to extend his suzerainty from the Caspian Sea to the

Aegean and from the shores of the Black Sea to the Persian Gulf, were foretold by the prophet as part of a divine plan. Whether Cyrus recognized it or not, he was breaking not only the shackles of political servitude but, and this of greater significance, the shackles of spiritual bondage which held men's minds in thrall as well. The fame of his generous policies did in fact "ungird the loins of kings," and many a mighty city surrendered without a battle at his approach. An original document, the Cyrus Cylinder, describes the conquest of Babylon in 539 B.C. as a peaceful occupation, with minor skirmishes at Oppis and Borshippa, and its claims are, in the main, supported by the Nabonidus Chronicle, which describes the same events from the point of view of the defeated foe.

That the establishment of the Persian Empire had sweeping consequences for the religious history of mankind is widely recognized. The following comment from Edward Meyer is much to the point:

"The two-hundred-year duration of the Persian Empire is a turning point for the whole history of religion. The national structure of the political life was finished for the world of the Near East, once religion had been loosed from state and politics. This created the individualism and universalism which from there on form the main trait of all religions. The task of the deity is no longer to protect the separate community, nor the state based upon a particular people, but it has become a universal, cosmic power, which addresses itself no longer to the totality of a people, but to the individual."[4]

Whether Cyrus was acquainted with the religious teaching of Zoroaster is a moot question. The references to Marduk and other gods of Babylon in the Cyrus Cylinder may be interpreted as a matter of political expediency. Though a monotheist at heart, Cyrus might feel tolerant toward the beliefs of other people. But no political expediency explains his generous policy toward the insignificant Jewish community in exile. As Moortgat aptly remarks: "There are few instances in the course of history, in which one perceives so clearly the guiding hand of a historical Providence, as by the decree which Cyrus issued from Ecbatana in 538, shortly after his occupation of Babylon, and by which he allowed the politically insignificant colony of Jewish exiles in Babylon to return to their home and gave them back the vessels of the temple which had been taken away."[5]

Persian King Cyrus restores religious treasures plundered by Babylon. Anointed by God, this king set forces in motion which marked a turning point for the whole history of religion. Engraving by Gustave Doré. Bettmann Archive.

That the ascendancy of Persia marked a decisive forward step in the political and moral history was keenly sensed by Ranke. "The monarchy of Persia fulfills a high mission. It has other aims in view than mere conquest and plunder. It rises far above the cruel Assyrian monarchy. For the divinities of Iran, pure and shining ones like the hosts of heaven, demand neither hecatombs nor rites of prostitution. . . . If they make war, it is not from motives of ambition, but to triumph over the powers of evil, to assure the final victory of the god of life. . . . That which contributes to the elevation of Darius is that his opponent's claim was based on falsehood. The protection which Ahura Mazda lends him he traces to the fact that he is the true king before whom the kings of falsehood must needs be overthrown. . . . Royal authority thus obtains a moral significance to which the whole structure of the kingdom and the state must be made to conform."[6]

Whether a disciple of Zoroaster or not, Cyrus was the free agent of a divine providence to set in motion influences which would promote the cause of freedom everywhere. His consistent abstention from wanton massacre of defenseless population proclaimed better than words his belief in human dignity and worth. The conviction slowly crystallized that the individual is significant and that he has a moral role to play in the triumph of good over evil.

According to E. Herzfeld, Zoroaster must have lived about 570-500 B.C.[7] If so, he would have been a contemporary of Cyrus. There was a persistent tradition that he lived 258 years before the era of Alexander, an opinion shared by A. V. Williams Jackson and most other modern historians.[8]

Darius's trilingual inscription carved on the rock of Behistun marks him as the first Persian monarch to worship Ahura-Mazda. His characterization of the usurper Gaumata as the king of 'Lie' may be interpreted as an effort to legitimize his claim to the throne by siding with the power of truth and labeling his opponent a champion of Angra Mainyu, the father of lies. "To Darius . . . Ahura-Mazda is he 'who created this earth, who created yonder heaven, who created man, who created welfare for man,' who gave the kingdom to his house and defends his empire from evil."[9]

Two generations later, however, Artaxerxes II (404-358 B.C.) seems to have abandoned the pure faith, for in one inscription he invokes besides Ahura Mazda, Anahita, the goddess of fertility, identified with the Babylonian Ishtar, and Mithra, a divine figure from old Aryan mythology who was destined to gain a belated popularity under the Roman Empire. Mankind's groping after light was at best a faltering pilgrimage.

A. C. Bouquet summarizes the tenets of Zoroaster's teaching[10] as follows: "Man's life is a good and precious thing, and each human being, man or woman, is responsible for making the most of it. Life is full of temptations and surrounded by perils, but it is nevertheless inspired by a good purpose. Wisdom personified is Lord of all, creator and judge, and will sometime in the future triumph over all opposition and reign supreme, giving to each human soul its just due. The object of human life is to work together with this beneficent deity, and to put one's self entirely at his service in the fight against evil; and his character is declared to be one of truth, social righteousness and justice."[11]

Zoroaster did not succeed in explaining the origin of evil, and although his ambiguity on this point gave occasion to later dualistic speculations, some historians regard it unfair to charge him with dualism.[12] He believed in good and bad spirits, or angels, but the stress is on the final triumph of good over evil, with man's responsibility to side with the forces of good in order to hasten its victory. This concept lends dignity and worth to human life. Man is confronted with moral choices which presuppose freedom. All of this marked a decided advance over the religious climate prevailing in Babylon where fate tended to paralyze all moral effort.

There is no evidence of a wholesale desertion from polytheism during the days of the Achmaenian empire. On the contrary, after Artaxerxes II, in their inscriptions even the kings of Persia reverted to the invocation of many gods, partly we may surmise, as a matter of expediency. But the religion of Zoroaster quickened man's thoughts even in distant Greece, where Herodotus, Plato, and others quote him by name. No smaller was its influence upon the Jewish communities in Babylon and in Palestine which under its stimulus produced a rich apocalyptic literature just before the dawn of the Christian era, in which the incipient dualism of Zoroaster finds a more complete expression. The polarity of light and darkness, truth and error, good and evil angels, becomes a constant refrain in this literature.

Another phenomenon of Neo-Babylonian and Persian times was the diffusion of the Aramaic language, which, in virtue of its simplicity, became the *lingua franca* of the Near East and the chief vehicle of culture in the days prior to Alexander's conquests. In postexilic times the Hebrew language had also given ground to Aramaic, and already Ezra needed the assistance of interpreters to make the law understandable to the Jewish community in Jerusalem. As shown by the Elephantine papyri discovered at the turn of this century, even Jews stationed in the distant colony of Elephantine in Upper Egypt were using the versatile Aramaic. This breakdown of the language barrier within the confines of the empire, together with the ensuing cultural amalgamation, was no insignificant part of that *praeparatio evangelica* leading up to the coming of Christ in "the fullness of time."

NOTES AND REFERENCES

1. Isaiah 45:1.
2. See Isaiah 44:28.
3. See E. Voegelin, *Order and History,* Vol. 1, p. 41.
4. Edward Meyer, *Ursprung and Anfange des Christentums,* Vol. 2, pp. 17-19. This passage is also commented upon by E. Herzfeld, in *Zoroaster and His World,* Vol. 1, p. 29.
5. Anton Moortgat, *Geschichte Vorderasiens bis zum Hellenismus, in Agypten and Vorderasien im Altertum,* pages 468, 469.
6. H. Ranke, *Universal History,* page 106.
7. E. Herzfeld, *op. cit.,* p. 30.
8. See A. V. Williams Jackson, *Zoroaster the Prophet of Ancient Iran,* pages 150 ff. For a different opinion see H. S. Nyberg, *Die Religionen des Alten Iran,* and W. F. Albright, *From the Stone Age to Christianity,* page 359.
9. G. B. Gray and M. Cary in *Cambridge Ancient History,* Vol. 4, *The Persian Empire and the West,* p. 210.
10. Since Zoroaster's teachings were not reduced to writing until late in Parthian times, and were not canonized until 300 A.D. under the Sasanian Dynasty, it is difficult to distinguish between the genuine teachings of the prophet and later accretions. On linguistic evidence, the Gathas seem to form the oldest stratum of the Avesta, and are thought to contain the purest form of Zoroastrianism.
11. A. C. Bouquet, *Man and Deity,* page 173.
12. This is the opinion of J. H. Moulton, followed by E. D. Soper, *The Religions of Mankind,* pages 142, 143.

Chapter 9

The Fullness of Time

A deep-rooted conviction of the apostle Paul was that God's revelation in Christ took place "when the time had fully come."[1] God's redemptive plan "to unite all things" in Christ was "a plan for the fullness of time."[2] All previous history had been preparatory for this event when eternity broke into time; it could not be ushered in until the stage had been fully set.

All history, particularly the tumultuous age beginning with the conquests of Alexander, was moving inexorably toward the advent of Christ. During the Hellenistic Age it unfolds at a swifter tempo. Crisis follows crisis. Not only are geographical lines erased, redrawn, and erased again, but linguistic and cultural barriers are hurled down as the nations of the Mediterranean basin coalesce into one world, the *oikoumenē*. Persia under Cyrus and Darius had unified the nations of the Near East into one empire, of which Aramaic was the chief language of cultural exchange.

For all its might the Persian Empire lacked internal cohesiveness. It was no more than a congeries of diverse peoples held together by clever administration and obvious military might. Yet even before Alexander, the ferment of change was introducing some homogeneity into these disparate peoples. Contacts with the higher Greek civilization became more common, resulting from armed conflicts for the control of the Aegean or peaceful penetration of commerce and ideas. No less effective was the ubiquitous presence of Greek mercenary troops in Persia fighting for the highest bidder, whether to reestablish native control in Egypt or to support Cyrus the Younger against his brother Arsikas for the throne. Greek artists invited to work in the royal palaces of Persepolis and Ecbatana, also acted as gadflies to the Persian colossus. Even before Alexander invaded, Hellenic art was conquering Persia.

After a brief flourish under the first Achaemenian kings, the religion of Zoroaster retreated into obscurity, but not without leavening religious thought everywhere with its lofty concept of God's nature and man's role in the final triumph over the forces of darkness.

The Jewish religious community in Palestine enjoyed two centuries of relative peace from the days of Ezra in the late fifth century to the Maccabean Age. During this period pious hands collected the precious literary legacy of the prophets, which came gradually to be regarded as canonical. Deprived of political independence since the Babylonian exile, the Jewish nation became a church which drew its inspiration and vitality from a Book. When, under the Seleucid kings, Hellenizing influences had become all but overwhelming, the Canon for all practical purposes had already been closed. The Hebrew nation's conviction of being a chosen people developed into adamant exclusivism, which became a butt of scorn to outsiders. Yet in its uncompromising adherence to the law, this little nation with its unrivaled religious blessing maintained its identity in the age of syncretism that followed on Alexander's heels.

If the dormant East underwent inevitable changes in its political and religious outlook even in the days of the Persian Empire, such changes were accelerated a hundredfold when Greece, under the Macedonian Alexander, swept through. In Alexander the world was confronted for the first time by an intention not only to conquer but to change the face of the earth. Tutored by Aristotle, heir to the best philosophical traditions of Greece and, on his father's side, to the best military machine of the day, Alexander presented a decisive challenge. Warring factions in the Greek city-states galvanized their energies toward a common goal, the conquest of the Persian Empire, but also, on a higher plane, toward cementing the nations of the Near East under the aegis of Hellenistic culture.

The military side of the grand design was quickly achieved. The heterogeneous hordes of Persia, without adequate leadership or motivation, were no match for the highly trained Macedonian armies led by one of the most gifted military commanders the world has ever seen.

In a series of swift maneuvers Alexander defeated the Persian defenders of Asia Minor at the river Granicus; at Issus he encountered the motley army of Darius III, caught it deployed stupidly in a narrow pass, and cut it to pieces; and, after the peaceful annexation of Egypt, he fought the third and decisive battle at Arbela in 331 B.C. Darius escaped only to be murdered shortly by his own officers. The next ten years Alexander spent both in mopping up resistance in the eastern satrapies of the new empire and in planting colonies from Egypt to India. Returning in 323 B.C. to Babylon, which he planned to make the capital of his far-flung empire, wearied by numberless skirmishes and interminable marches, frustrated by the complexities of administering so immense a territory, Alexander contracted a fever and died at the age of thirty-three.

That his grandiose design of Hellenizing the East did not collapse at his death is to be explained not only by the military competence of his generals, but also by the remarkable degree to which Alexander's plan met the aspirations of the new age. In the absence of qualified heirs, unity of the empire could not be preserved. After the battle of Ipsus in 301, in which Antigonus was defeated and killed, the empire was divided among the victorious generals as follows: Ptolemy retained Egypt which he already controlled, Seleucus received Syria and the satrapies to the east including Babylon, Lysimachus fell heir to Thrace and Asia Minor, and Cassander took Macedonia. On the ever-changing political chessboard, two dynasties managed to survive over two hundred years: The Seleucids remained in Syria until Pompey occupied it in 63 B.C., and the Ptolemies lasted in Egypt down to 30 B.C., when Octavian made Egypt a Roman province.

Cultural unity transcended these artificial political boundaries. Versatile Greek displaced Aramaic as the common language or *lingua franca* of the Near East and became the chief vehicle for the exchange of ideas in the entire Mediterranean world. Many of the Greek colonies established by Alexander prospered and became foci for the diffusion of Hellenism in the East. Chief among these, Alexandria in Egypt under the Ptolemies displaced Athens as the center of Hellenistic culture. Under royal patronage its museum and library became a center of literary and scientific activity. What the Alexandrian literati lacked in originality they made up in industriousness, preserving and critically analyzing the literary heritage from the classical age. In the sciences the Greeks of Alexandria, Syracuse, and Pergamum went beyond anything their forebears had achieved. Euclid systematized geometry in the form it would retain for the next two thousand years, Eratosthenes measured the circumference of the earth, and Archimedes discovered the specific gravity of bodies.

The ruins of Sebaste, Scythopolis, Philadelphia, Gerasa, Petra, Baalbek, Dura-Europos, to mention a few, testify to the prevalence of Greek style in urbanism and architecture throughout the Near East. Cities in a splurge of wealth vied with each other for the most beautiful amphitheaters, marketplaces, temples, and colonnaded avenues. Antiochia even boasted a public illumination system. No city was considered civilized without its own gymnasium and palaestra. Athletic games became fashionable even in culturally backward Palestine. Greek art and thought radiated as far as India and China. Hellenistic *oikoumenē* was indeed becoming one world.

One effect was the breakdown of the narrow loyalty of the city-state, particularly in Greece. In an expanding economy the city-state political system had outlived its usefulness. It was, in fact, the unwillingness or incapacity of the Greeks to recognize this historical fact that plunged Greece into the fratricidal Peloponnesian War of the late fifth century, from which Athens never fully recovered. The psychosis of fear following this war together with Athenian inability to diagnose its own ills culminated in the judicial murder of Socrates which, in the opinion of A. J. Toynbee, contributed more than anything else "to detach Hellenic hearts from all city-states."[3] Another factor in the emancipation of individuals from the *polis* were the plays of Euripides who, by discrediting the old Olympian religion, undermined the prestige of the gods under whose aegis the city-states had thrived.

Considering that the city-states long gave the average citizen full scope for the exercise of his political and social aspirations, the disappearance of the traditional loyalties was in this sense a loss. The *polis* had conferred on each citizen a sense of belonging, clearly staking out for each his role within a close-knit community. On the other hand, parochialism had to be broken if individuals were to realize their full potentiality in the new *oikoumenē*. Cast adrift in the great sea of competing world views and religious outlooks, the individual must rethink life's meaning within a much vaster frame of reference. Readjustment from a provincial outlook, with answers for all major questions neatly handed down from generation to generation, to a wider world brimming over with unanswered questions was bound to be painful. But though painful, the readjustment was part of a providential schooling that would bring man closer to a knowledge of himself and God.

The Hellenistic Age helped bring out the individual in a cosmopolitan culture. By creating a world community in which individuals and ideas moved well, due to the wonderfully pliant Greek *koinē* and the infections élan of Hellenistic culture, Hellenism triumphed over the isolationism of the city-state. Thus it became increasingly impossible for any one city to ignore for very long the changing world beyond its horizon. Sooner or later it was drawn into the political and cultural maelstrom and amalgamated with Hellenism. The corporate personality of the city-state with which people were identified from birth to death gave way to cosmopolitanism in whose impersonal bosom each individual must survive on his own. Cut loose from the umbilical cord of the *polis,* the individual must now live in an environment that seemed to him threatening and unpredictable. Cast on his own, the individual must find answers to the pressing problems of life, whether economic, cultural, or religious. And the answers he found were not necessarily those of his ancestors. In fact, they were bound to be as different as the new world view imposed on him was different. And most significant, the agony of reappraisal provided God's opportunity to awaken in man a deeper sense of helplessness and his need of a Redeemer from the thralldom of sin and meaninglessness. In that bewildering age men were, as the poet has said,

> Wandering between two worlds, one dead,
> The other powerless to be born.

Of the soul-searching agony of this age of transition S. Angus wrote: "By the failure of collective responsibility in the city-state the individual responsibility was augmented to an extent perplexing to the average man. The emergence of this brooding sense of failure, the consciousness of sin and its ineluctable moral issues, the bewilderment of individualism, were the moral counterpart of the great social upheavals."[4]

Unwittingly Alexander and his successors were propelling the world to a higher stage of political and moral freedom. In this sense, then, their historical mission may be said to have been providential. Political ambitions on the part of some great personalities turned out to be the lever whereby Providence was moving mankind toward a greater measure of freedom and its concomitant responsibility. Indeed, no significant progress in man's groping after God was possible in a climate inimical to individual responsibility. As long as man felt himself sheltered within the bulwark of time-honored political and religious institutions, his sense of individual dependence upon God tended to atrophy. In matters religious no delegation of responsibility is allowable. Man must first stand alone before God before any collective standing can be meaningful. The upheavals of the Hellenistic Age were agencies whereby men were drawn out as individuals from the confinement of the clan or the city-state to have a personal confrontation with God. And being liberated from parochial loyalties, man became for the first time aware of that wider community of mankind in which "there is neither Jew nor Greek, there is neither slave nor free, there is neither male nor female,"[5] for in God all are one.

Alexander's role in introducing into the world the new ideas of human brotherhood finds expression in W. W. Tarn's remark: "These [new ideas] originated on the day—one of the critical moments of history—when, at banquet at Opis, Alexander prayed for a union of hearts (*homonoia*) and a joint commonwealth of Macedonians and Persians; he was the first to transcend national boundaries and to envisage, however imperfectly, a brotherhood of man in which there should be neither Greek nor barbarian."[6]

In his *Hellenistic Religions* F. C. Grant gives us this synopsis of the Hellenistic Age: "A single world language, a single homogeneous universal culture, and a worldwide centripetal tendency observable in the political realm—all this encouraged a general tendency toward monotheism and a common longing for salvation. Never in history had questions about God and His nature been so widely discussed. . . . Indeed, the whole Hellenistic age, after the disillusioned and cynical fourth century, and especially after the bitter third and second centuries, was in increasing measure a religious age."[7]

Expressions of the religious aspirations of the age can be collected from hundreds of pagan epitaphs as well as from the pages of pagan authors, such as, for example, the following statement from Seneca: "There is some great Deity, and greater than can be imagined; and for Him we endeavor to live. Let us approve ourselves to Him. For it is no avail that conscience is confined; we lie open to the sight of God."[8] Who does not feel the pathos of Plutarch's words: "The hope of immortality and the hope of existence are the most venerable and the mightiest of all affections"?[9] And Lucretius characterized a whole age when he wrote, "In the days of adversity the minds of men turn more eagerly toward religion."[10]

What could the Hellenistic world offer to satisfy man's religious quest? In Greece the Olympian gods were nearly dead. As Tarn puts it, "Philosophy killed them for the educated, individualism for the common man."[11] Through ridicule the sophists of the Periclean age had driven them to the realm of superstition. Forms of the ancient cult were indeed maintained as props of the city-states, but with their disintegration even the forms disappeared. New temples, if erected at all, were generally dedicated to some alien deity like Serapis of Alexandria. After four centuries the temple of Apollo at Didyma was still unfinished, not for lack of resources, but for lack of living faith which had inspired previous generations to begin it.

Socrates's single-handed struggle with the sophists was not to save the Olympian gods to whom he continued to pay lip service, but to awaken the Greek conscience. By focusing his inquisitive mind on man rather than on nature, he gave a new orientation to Greek philosophical thought. Against the moral relativism taught by the sophists, Socrates propounded that truth will invariably lead to goodness. Possessed of a deep moral sense, he refused to escape from duty and death. None who came to know this gadfly of the Athenian conscience could ever remain indifferent to the claims of his better self. But conscience, once launched on the quest for moral excellence, could never be satisfied with what either pagan religion or philosophy could offer. Once man has seen the glorious vision, says de Pressensé, "he knows that he has failed to fulfill the law of his being, and an aspiration never to be quenched is awakened in his heart, after full deliverance from evil. The desire to attain to this will keep him in a state of constant unrest and will deepen his aspiration after the unknown God in whom all the prophetic intuitions of his soul are to be realized."[12]

Socrates was the tutor of Plato, in whom religious mysticism and philosophy blended in a rare combination. Plato's notion that the visible world of things was but a temporal shadow of the eternal realm of pure ideas was to have an indelible influence on Christian theology through Posidonius and Plotinus. Several early Christian apologists, including Clement, Justin Martyr, and Origen, felt that Greek philosophy had been one of the agencies Providence used to pave the way for Christianity. Clement quotes the apocryphal *Preaching of Peter* as proving that one eternal God "known to the Greeks in a Gentile fashion and to the Jews in a Jewish fashion and to us in a new and spiritual fashion" was "the Giver of Greek philosophy to the Greeks," which he believed to be one of the two divine antecedents of Christianity.[13] In the words of A. de Pressensé: "Socrates and Plato fulfilled a truly sublime mission in their day and nation. They were the great prophets of the human conscience in the pagan world. The world awoke at their call, and this quickening of the moral sense was at once the glory and the death of philosophy under its systematic form; for conscience, once aroused from its torpor, failed to find its full satisfaction in philosophy."[14]

Several attempts were made, nevertheless, to formulate a satisfying philosophy to serve as guide in a perplexing world. Chief among these was the philosophical system taught by Zeno, the founder of the Stoic school. His system, like that of Epicurus, aimed not at speculating about truth as such, but at providing practical guidance for the individual in his earthly pilgrimage. The goal was individual happiness through moral conduct. Both schools recognized unsatisfied desire as the root of unhappiness, and, therefore, pointed to the negation of passions and emotions as the road to happiness. Both stressed the importance of morality apart from politics. But whereas for the Stoics virtue had value for its own sake, for the Epicureans virtue was a means to happiness. Happiness was equated with the maximum of pleasure, not the physical and sensual pleasures lauded by the Cyrenaics, but intellectual pleasure, for the mind was man's noblest possession.

The Stoics conceived mankind as one great brotherhood and the universe as one great city ruled by one supreme power, whom they indifferently called Destiny, Providence, or Nature. From this power of divine fire came all that exists including man's soul, which to them was in a derivative sense divine. History was conceived as cyclical, the universe at the end of every world cycle being reabsorbed into the divine fire. The Stoics' god, scarcely distinguishable from universal law, is, paradoxically, thought of as a moral god whose design was all-wise and all-good. "Still everything was determined; and," as W. W. Tarn points out, "in determinism the Stoics encountered the usual difficulty, for first and foremost their system was a moral one, and without free will there could be no morality."[15] A second difficulty was how to explain inequalities among men, patent for all to see, when all were citizens of the same world-empire.

The solution to the first dilemma was found in the concept of duty. Man was free, but it was his duty to subordinate his will to the divine will, so to live as to lead his thoughts captive to the divine mind, whose purposes, after all, envisaged his own happiness. Instead of kicking against the pricks, it was his privilege to identify his mind with the mind of God and thus live at peace. If the glad acceptance of duty ensured peace of mind, the practice of virtue, which meant absolute harmony with the all-virtuous supreme power, was the sure way to happiness. If luxury and sensual pleasure, wealth and success, were no part of the divine plan, then their enjoyment was a matter of indifference. For them even the loss of a dear one should be no source of grief, for the decrees of God were all-wise.

The problem of inequality among men was solved by affirming that such inequalities as existed affected only the body and not the soul. Since the human body was mere clay, it mattered nothing. In the realm of the soul even the beggar might be king, and the free was not better off than the slave. In sum, Stoicism offered salvation here and now by self-realization and self-reliance. Stoicism appealed to the strong athletic souls, and its affinities with Roman moral virtues won to it such noble adherents as Epictetus and Marcus Aurelius. "But," as S. Angus remarks, "all men are not of the heroic temperament and few are capable of becoming experts in philosophy, and fewer still are able to bring their philosophic convictions to bear upon the conduct of life."[16] For all its noble concepts of duty and virtue, Stoicism lacked the dynamic to translate ideals into actual life. Worse yet, says Tarn, "it had no place for love, and it scarcely met the misery of the world to tell the slave in the mines that if he would only think aright he would be happy."[17] In spite of its shortcomings, Stoicism was the noblest product of pagan philosophy, and it may be termed in the words of Winkler a "root of Christianity." It also acted as pedagogue in leading men to Christ who alone could infuse their ethics with love and hope. Its insistance on the things of the soul, or character, as man's only and inalienable possession, found some agreement in the pages of the New Testament.

If philosophy provided a measure of moral guidance and comfort to an intellectual minority, the mystery religions did it for the common man. The cult of Dionysius had seen some votaries in Greece even in preclassic days, but it attained surprising popularity after the Olympian gods fell into disrepute. Basic to all mystery religions, whether Greek or Oriental, was the idea of *soteria,* "salvation," by personal identification with a savior-god who had himself died and risen again. The myth of a dying and rising god was suggested by the annual life cycle, which presented to man's wondering eyes the ever-thrilling spectacle of the rebirth of nature in the spring after the desolation of winter. To its votaries in Mesopotamia the rising god was Dumuzi; in Egypt, Osiris; in Canaan, Baal; in later Phoenicia, Adonis. Each of these finds parallels in Dionysius of Hellas. The rebirth of nature in the spring suggested powerfully to wistful man the possibility that he, too, might live again after death and thus fulfill his fondest dream.

However much they might differ in detail, the mystery religions had this in common: The bliss of immortality was vouchsafed only to those admitted to the rite of initiation. Their ceremonies were as a rule performed at night, or at least in a dark temple. Here the mystic was called by the deity and awakened to a new life. He experienced *soteria,* or redemption, which involved a deep transformation of his inner being. He underwent what was known as *anagenesis,* "transformation," or *paligenesia,* a spiritual "new birth." From that moment on he received "illumination" through secret wisdom. The details of such rites are practically unknown from the extant literature, partially because the devotees pledged secrecy under oath. In Hellenistic times the ancient mystery religions, whether Dionysiac, Orphic, Eleusinian, or Anatolian, adjusted themselves to man's deepening sense of sin and the need of deliverance not only from the power of death but from the terrors of astral determinism and fate.

Although some mystery cults were crude and orgiastic, others were dignified. Some condoned magic; others offered a greater ethical appeal. Their vitality lay in the fact that they fulfilled some basic human aspirations, prominent among which was the sense of belonging. Uprooted men found in the mystic religious fraternities that social warmth which official religion no longer provided. In fact, the mysteries did much to obliterate all social and economic barriers by declaring that in matters religious all men stood on equal footing. Their influence was on the side of denationalizing religion and making it a matter of personal choice. Man was given the option of choosing the faith he would live by. Garbled under pagan trappings, this faith echoed certain Biblical truths, such as the possibility of a mystic union with the Deity.[18]

God used the mystery religions to promote His own ends. In the language of S. Angus: "They fostered new and profound religious cravings and stirred up high hopes which Christianity alone could adequately satisfy. . . . They supplied Christianity in its Hellenistic mission field with a soteriological vocabulary and ideas which proved both fruitful and of lasting value.[19]

If notions derived from the mystery cults such as esoteric privileges in religion and the stress on ritual and sacramentarianism later warped patristic Christianity and almost made it a mystery religion, the blame lies with man's slow grasp of the religion of Christ which burst the worn-out skins of the mystery cults. They were among the diverse systems which in their own distorted ways managed to render service in their own time but were superseded by the Christian revelation.

If Greek philosophy and the mystery religions in both their Western and Oriental garbs offered partial answers to man's religious quest, Judaism was in a position to offer an infinitely better spiritual refuge. The reason its spiritual outreach was less than effective is not found in any intrinsic inadequacy, but in the narrow exclusivism of its votaries. As the prophets had pointed out, one of the purposes of the Babylonian captivity was to shatter the fetters of religious exclusivism. Yet despite the captivity it remained a national religion, a light hidden under a bushel.

The dictum often repeated—that Israel went to exile as a nation and returned to the Promised Land as a church—falls far short of the truth. The teachings of Amos on God's concern for all peoples, of Jeremiah on religion as a matter of the heart independent of temple and ritual, of Ezekiel on individual accountability before God, or of Isaiah on God's house being called "a house of prayer for all peoples,"[20] fell largely on deaf ears. There is little evidence that the community which returned from the Babylonian exile were possessed of any greater missionary zeal than their forebears. Israel's mission to become "a light to the nations"[21] was never apprehended by more than a few.

In spite of ingrained bigotry, Israel, as the bearer of divine oracles and recipient of divine promises, would not be allowed permanently to keep its spiritual legacy hidden from the world at large. In the Hellenistic Age, the prospect of material advantages in the new cities founded by Alexander and the Diadochi led to a gradual dispersion of the Jews throughout the *oikoumenē*. The Jews of the Diaspora formed greater or smaller nuclei in every major city of the Mediterranean world. It has been estimated that by the time of Nero one in every seven inhabitants of the empire was a Jew. The estimate may be exaggerated, but the wandering Jew was a conspicuous figure in the Hellenistic world, and Jewish synagogues were erected everywhere.

In spite of himself, the Jew's religious practices and views came to be known far and wide. A tombstone from Rheneia on the island of Delos, dated from 100 B.C., bears mute witness to "God the Most High, Lord of the spirits and all flesh," and makes unequivocal reference to the Day of Atonement.[22] Educated pagans, even though mistakenly ascribing to it a philosophical or pantheistic character, left favorable comments on Jewish worship. Others were impressed by Jewish monotheism and the absence of images in their cult. Among such were Theophrastus and Clearchus, disciples of Aristotle, as well as Varro and Strabo, both probably influenced by Posidonius. The quiet religious propaganda of the Jews disturbed the Gentiles, as is shown by the growing anti-Semitism in literature after 100 B.C. But anti-Jewish feeling may be only part of that general reaction in the West against Oriental invasion, be it in the realm of religion or of business, in which to the chagrin of their Gentile neighbors the Jews often had a lion's share. Philo's and Josephus's apologies, meant to allay Gentile misunderstanding of peculiar Jewish ways and to contest the charge that Jews had contributed nothing to culture, glossed over the features objectionable to Gentiles, such as circumcision, and minimized real differences between the Greek and Jewish world views.

Of incalculable consequence for the future of Judaism and Christianity was the translation of the Hebrew Old Testament into Greek for the benefit of the Jews of the Diaspora who no longer used their native tongue. The need of such a translation was greatest in Alexandria, where the numerous Jewish population felt as nowhere else the impact of Hellenistic culture. As early as the days of Ptolemy Philadelphus (309 - 246 B.C.) the pentateuch was translated into Greek, and within a century the translation of the whole Old Testament was probably completed. The Greek Septuagint version kept millions in the old faith, to win fresh millions for whom the Hebrew text would have remained a buried treasure. Or, as Deissman aptly remarks, "Greek Judaism with the Septuagint had ploughed the furrows for the gospel seed in the Western world."[23] The Septuagint was in fact the first and for a long time the only Bible of incipient Christianity.

The original exclusivism of Judaism lost much of its edge in contact with the wider Hellenistic world. That the Jewish Diaspora should permanently escape the pressure of foreign religious and cultural influences was not to be expected and was perhaps not in the best interest of mankind. The Jewish apocryphal literature which came to existence in the two centuries before the Christian era shows in a marked degree, both in content and literary style, Hellenistic influences. The sharp contrast between the matter-of-fact style of First Maccabees, which stays close to the facts, and the legendary and rhetorical color of Second Maccabees, is a case in point. The apocryphal "Wisdom of Solomon," which dates probably from the reign of Alexander Jannaeus (102 - 76 B.C.), makes Wisdom the mediator between God and man. It is shot through with Platonic ideas such as the body's being merely a shell for the soul which is inherently immortal.

The greatest single-handed effort to make the Jewish faith palatable to the Greek mind was that of Philo of Alexandria. It is a moot question whether Philo was ever consciously overstepping the boundaries of Judaism with his speculations. That he bent backward to accommodate Greek views is evident from his biography of Moses, in which he identifies his hero with the ideal of Wisdom. By his allegorical method he tries to make Jewish religious practices, such as circumcision and animal sacrifices, as well as Jewish history, less offensive to his Greek readers. He admits skepticism as a prerequisite of a higher form of mystical knowledge. In his philosophical system, partly borrowed from Posidonius, he makes allowance for a sharp dualism between God and the world, which he bridges by the concept of the Logos, and offers an ethic which attempts to blend the ascetic tendencies of Platonism with the Stoic principle of life "according to nature."[24] In spite of his syncretism, he manages to retain the idea that the Scripture is the fountain of all wisdom and that in a superlative way its history and its law reflect the best in Greek philosophical thought. The concept of the Logos, for example, finds its counterpart in the hypostatized concept of the Word of God, just as natural law is analogical to the Mosaic *Torah*. Though exalting the "spiritual" meaning of the Scriptures above the literal, Philo wants to preserve both, at least insofar as the law is concerned. For him its precepts remain unchanged as long as "sun and moon and the whole heaven and the world stand."

There is little evidence that Philo exerted much influence over his contemporaries.[25] In the xenophobic reaction following the destruction of Jerusalem in A.D. 70, Palestinian Jewry turned its back on Philo and similar attempts to compromise the faith.

More effective in paving the way for Christianity was the quiet propaganda radiating from the synagogues of the Jewish Diaspora, lay institutions which kept alive the old faith without the priests and sacrifices of the temple. Their strength derived from an unswerving loyalty to the Scriptures, the reading of which, together with prayer, formed the core of the simple religious service celebrated every Sabbath. In the broad competitive world the Jewish faith lost much of its narrow particularism, and the doors of the synagogues were thrown open to Gentiles attracted by its sublime monotheism and its strong ethical stand. Proselytes were won in great numbers, and sympathizers came to be known as "God-fearers." A reference to this earnest religious propaganda is found in Matthew 23:15. Flavius Josephus tells of the Jewish merchant Ananias who converted King Izates of Adiabene and his wife to the Jewish faith. Yet even this flowering of proselytizing zeal was cut short by the anti-Hellenistic reaction which swept Palestine and infected the Diaspora following the Jewish wars erupting under Nero and Hadrian.

It was nonetheless among these proselytes and sympathizers that the missionary activity of Paul and other apostles achieved its best results. Schooled by Jewish tutors and yet unfettered by age-old particularism, such enlightened Gentiles were quick to discern in the gospel message the fulfillment of all that had been foreshadowed "in the law and the prophets."

For those engaged in founding Christian churches during the apostolic age, both the early forcible Babylonian exile of the Jews and their later voluntary dispersion throughout the Hellenistic world in the days of Alexander and his successors bore evidence of an overruling providence. The participants in the drama may not have been aware of the spiritual mission they were called to perform, but the presence of synagogues—with their adherents and "God-fearers"—from Dura-Europos on the Euphrates to Carthagena in Spain quietly preparing the Gentile soil for the seed of the gospel had incalculable consequences for the future of the church.

The synagogues did more than serve as preparatory schools for the thousands of Gentiles attracted through their persuasive monotheism and lofty moral code. The Christian church would be likewise indebted to the synagogue for its form of worship in which the reading of the Scriptures was central, for its primitive hymnology, and for congregational participation in prayer and responsive reading of Scripture, as well as for that measure of local initiative and responsibility in sustaining the faith which distinguished the synagogues. Above all, the converted Jews deserve the credit for infusing the incipient Christian churches with a noble sense of moral worth. In the words of Dobschütz: "The Jewish Christianity . . . trained by the law was, so to speak, the backbone which supported the moral tone of the whole. We must never forget that Paul himself was sprung from Judaism. And the Judaistic agitation in his churches, in spite of all the injury it did, still achieved the result of laying more stress on the moral side of Christianity."[26]

In the days of Antiochus IV, while the Jews of the Diaspora were leading a quiet life, only occasionally agitated by localized persecuting

Mattathias kills Greek for profaning temple. This fearless Jew led a band of guerrillas against the ruling Greeks in Palestine. Engraving by Gustave Doré. Historical Pictures Service, Chicago.

and steadily gaining in influence in both financial and political circles, the Jews of Palestine experienced a life-and-death struggle for survival. Up to then Hellenization had been a quiet leavening process supported by the Greco-Macedonian ruling houses, a process which owed much of its success to the fascination which a dazzling new culture exerted over urban populations throughout the Near East. Overawed barbarians everywhere aped Greek fashion in dress, architecture, and religion. A few itinerant preachers, propagating the views of the Cynic and Stoic philosophies, succeeded in creating clubs of like-minded citizens here and there. But Hellenism needed no propaganda, much less force, for its diffusion. Even so, Antiochus IV Epiphanes (215 - 163 B.C.), a passionate admirer of things Greek, tried to impose Hellenism by force upon his recalcitrant Jewish subjects. For his folly, wags named him Epimanes (madman).

To Antiochus, the title Epiphanes (manifest god) was no mere epithet. For personal or political reasons he took his divinity seriously, posing as Zeus, hoping to unify his kingdom in culture and in cult in order to be better able to cope with the Romans. When on the occasion of his second intervention in Egyptian affairs in 168 B.C. he was ordered out of the country by Popilius Loena, who was flushed with pride after the Roman victory at Pydna, Antiochus's chagrin knew no bounds. His emissary Apollonios stormed the city of Jerusalem, profaned the temple, and made the practice of the Jewish religion illegal. The Levitical sacrifices were suspended, and animals abominable to the Jews were offered on the altar. Circumcision and the observance of the Sabbath and other religious feasts were forbidden. Inspectors were sent to assure obedience to the decree in the countryside. In Jerusalem all the licenses of pagan worship were shamelessly installed, including the presence of *hierodules,* sacred prostitutes, in the courts of the temple, and the Dionysiac orgies were celebrated.

The reaction of the conservative element of the nation—who stood loyal to the old faith in opposition to enforced worship of Zeus Olympius promoted by Antiochus IV—is well known. The latent resentment of thousands was sparked into armed revolt when Mattathias, a priest who had taken refuge in Modin, not only refused to submit to the demand to offer a sacrifice to the pagan god, but cut down the royal officer who asked compliance. Certain of reprisals, Mattathias, his sons, and many sympathizers withdrew to mountain fastnesses to begin guerrilla warfare in self-defense, later turning it into a war of liberation from oppressive Syrian control. What followed was a series of unexpected victories in the face of overwhelming odds for the patriotic bands led by Judas Maccabaeus, son of Mattathias. The first army raised by Apollonios and made up of army regulars supported by a Samaritan contingent was roundly defeated, Appolonios losing his sword and his life to Judas. No less spectacular was the defeat suffered by a district general, Seron, who at Bethoron lost eight hundred men to Judas and his ragtag army. Next Judas would have to face the grim Antiochus himself, who was resolved to crush the rebellion.

But Antiochus was distracted by the Parthians, who threatened eastern provinces of his realm. The governor of Coela-Syria entrusted the task of subduing the Jewish rebels to a new army under the command of Nicanor, a favorite of the king, assisted by Gorgias. Once again, after reassuring his troops by the reading of the *Torah,* Judas surprised the Syrian army camped near Emmaus and won a resounding victory. After a series of prestige-damaging Syrian defeats, Lysias, acting as regent in the absence of Antiochus, took the field in person.

From his camp in Bethzur, eighteen miles south of Jerusalem, he saw in diplomacy rather than war the better part of wisdom. Lysias made several important concessions to the conservative Jewish party, and in December of 164 B.C., three years after the first sacrifice had been offered to Zeus Olympius, a new altar of burnt offerings had been erected and the temple purified from pagan defilement. The following year Antiochus IV, failing in the attempt to take the treasures of the temple of Elymas, died brokenhearted near Ispahen. Within two decades, under Jonathan and Simon, the Jewish nation had regained both religious and political freedom far beyond the most sanguine hopes of Mattathias and those who died for the defense of the faith in the early days of the war.

W. W. Tarn in his *Hellenistic Civilization,* after surveying Antiochus's vain attempts to introduce religious and cultural uniformity among his Jewish subjects, sardonically remarks that "though Judas played the part of patriot, what saved the worship of Yahweh was not his sword but Seleucid dissension."[27] The author apparently sides with those who view the remarkable victories of Judas and his compatriots against insuperable odds as one of those streaks of luck which "at one turning point after another, directed fortune its way." But to read the successes of the Maccabean revolt with their incalculable consequences for the future of Judaism and Christianity as the result of a streak of luck is willfully to write off meaning from history.

On the contrary, belief in a divine providence gently guiding the many possible alternatives following each human choice restores sense to what would be an idle tale "full of sound and fury signifying nothing." The very distractions, political and otherwise, which kept Antiochus from directing the full might of his realm against little Judea at this crucial moment are recognized by the believer as tokens of an overruling providence quietly presiding over the drama of history.

Bevan comes much closer to the providential view when he remarks: "Some modern scholars speak sarcastically of the Jewish books which represent the events in Judaea as the things of central importance in the world and pretend that Antiochus's chief preoccupation was the ill-success of the local government forces in dealing with Jewish bands. No doubt, from the point of view of Antiochus, the Jewish books greatly exaggerate the importance of events in Judaea, just as from the point of view of the Persian King, we may believe, the Greek books greatly exaggerated the importance of the battle of Marathon. In regard to the influence destined to be exerted upon the subsequent history of mankind, the Greek books and the Jewish books were right. Of all that was happening in the kingdom of Antiochus, the events in Judaea were by far the most important in their consequences for the mind of man in ages to come."[28]

The role of Judaism as a preparatory school for Christianity bears a striking resemblance to that of John the Baptist as the forerunner of Christ. Both had a historical mission to fulfill in the divine scheme. But whereas John, his mission completed, bowed out gracefully from the stage, deferring to Christ with the words, "He must increase, but I must decrease,"[29] Judaism as a whole failed to recognize the One to whom all symbols and prophecies pointed, and unwittingly exited from the stage at the most crucial point.

NOTES AND REFERENCES

1. Galatians 4:4.
2. Ephesians 1:10.
3. A. J. Toynbee, *Hellenism,* page 130.
4. S. Angus, *The Religious Quests of the Graeco-Roman World,* page 44.
5. Galatians 3:28.
6. W. W. Tarn, *Hellenistic Civilizations,* page 73.
7. F. C. Grant, *Hellenistic Religions,* page xxxii.
8. Seneca.
9. Plutarch, *Non posse suav.* 26.
10. Lucretius, *De rerum nat.* IIIc 53 f.
11. W. W. Tarn, *op. cit.,* p. 302.
12. A. de Pressensé, *The Ancient World and Christianity,* page 345.
13. *Stromata* VI. 5; 41, 6.
14. A. de Pressensé, *op. cit.,* p. 348.
15. W. W. Tarn, *op. cit.,* p. 297.
16. S. Angus, *op. cit.,* p. 66.
17. W. W. Tarn, *op. cit.,* p. 325.
18. Compare Erich Kahler, *The Meaning of History,* page 57.
19. S. Angus, *op. cit.,* p. 85.
20. Isaiah 56:6, 7.
21. Isaiah 42:6.
22. See Paul Wendland, *Die Hell-Römische Kultur,* page 194.
23. Deissman, *New Light on the Old Testament,* page 95.
24. See Paul Wendland, *op. cit.,* p. 204.
25. Whether his teaching colored the Christian literature of the second century is likewise open to doubt. Similarities of thought might be explained as direct borrowings from profane Platonism which was in vogue following its revival in the first century B.C.
26. E. von Dobschütz, *Christian Life in the Primitive Church,* page 172.
27. W. W. Tarn, *op. cit.,* p. 187.
28. E. R. Bevan, *The Cambridge Ancient History,* Vol. 8, pp. 513, 514.
29. John 3:30.

Chapter 10

Christianity Against Its Environment

Some circles entertain the notion that Christianity owed its triumph over pagan competitors to a fortuitous combination of favorable circumstances. Some might even conclude that Christianity rode to triumph on the strength of an ingenious syncretism of the best concepts entertained by Judaism and the mystery religions of the day, capitalizing on widespread apocalyptic expectations and a favorable political climate. The obvious conclusion, not always explicitly stated, is that no supernatural providence must be invoked to explain its success. If cogent historical causes can be adduced, it is alleged, then God is explained away from the process.

There are two fallacies in this type of reasoning. The first is the assumption that divine providence must be equated with the mysterious and unintelligible. If reason can be found in a colligation of events, it is then thought that God has nothing to do with the process. But why, we ask, should divine providence never operate in a way understandable to the human mind? Should it not be occasion for praise and gratitude when man can find out God's ways and think His thoughts after Him? There is no question that over and beyond man's highest reaches unfathomable mysteries still challenge men's minds through the ages. Yet it seems consistent with the Biblical concept of man created in God's image, capable of holding communion with his Creator, that, within the limits of man's finitude, God's ways should be intelligible to him. The operation of divine providence within the historical process should be at least partially discernible and capable of conveying meaning to man's mind. There is no justification for excluding divine providence from those areas of history in which systematic research has discovered patches of meaning. God is Lord of all history, both its intelligible and its enigmatic portions.

The second fallacy is associated with the notion of historical causation. Strictly speaking, historical events are never connected as links in a chain of cause and effect. To some degree history is open. Even in nature, since the recognition of the principle of indeterminacy, phenomena are no longer thought of as bound to each other in total cause and effect. Quantum physics dealt the deathblow to the principle of strict causality. The laws of nature are now best understood as laws of greater or lesser probability depending on the scale of the phenomena studied. If there is indeterminacy and openness in the microcosm of the atom, should we assume less openness in the sphere of history where the chief actor is the least predictable of all, man's will? In spite of its noncommittal nature, there is much truth in Edward Meyer's contention that "the proper object of historical thought is historical fact in its individuality, and that chance and free will are determining causes that cannot be banished from history without destroying its very essence."[1]

Wherever the noncommitted historian speaks of chance, the Christian with better reason may speak of divine providence. And wherever free will is admitted as operative, the notion of strict historical determinism must be discarded as meaningless. All the historian can talk about is the probability that event B may follow event A, and that such and such colligation of events makes sense. But the future is never unequivocally determined by the past, as the notion of historical causation might suggest. The historian may, then, study the factors which make a configuration of events intelligible. But having achieved this, he can never claim that the task he set for himself is completed once and for all. The task is adjudged well done if it appears convincing to fellow historians. Yet there lurks the possibility that a new generation of historians will not be satisfied.

The fact that each generation must rewrite past history to make it meaningful in terms of a new set of criteria, corroborates the conclusion that historical explanations are never final. This is tantamount to saying that there are no historical causes, strictly speaking, that the future is not wholly determined by the past, that novelty and change are of the essence of history, and that there are no cogent *a priori* reasons to deny an operative providence in the historical process.

It is customary to invoke the Messianic expectation in Jewish and pagan circles, the apocalyptic hopes entertained during the two centuries preceding the Christian era, the religious syncretism which amalgamated the best in the religious tradition of different peoples, and the inexorable trend toward monotheism as the reasons for Christianity's triumph, and then to assume that its victory was the "natural" and inevitable outcome of these historical antecedents. To these are added the superficial analogies between the mystery religions of Greece and the Orient and certain features of early Christianity in order to explain away the uniqueness of the Christ-event. And for good measure, since the discovery of the Dead-Sea Scrolls in 1947, certain practices of the Qumran community are stressed out of proportion to give the impression that the Christian church was patterned after the Essene rules.

Yet Christianity triumphed, not in a world waiting open-armed for such a divine revelation, not in hand-in-glove conformity with the religious aspirations of the day, but in the face of bitter opposition and misunderstanding. Discrediting neither the long-protracted historical preparation of mankind's groping after God through the maze of pagan darkness nor the calling of a "chosen people" to act as a catalyst of human longing after the divine, Christianity triumphed against its environment nevertheless. The Johannine verdict is that Christ "came unto His own, and His own received Him not."[2]

The weight of the New Testament witness uniformly emphasizes the antagonisms rather than the agreements between Christian and pagan mores and thought. It was not in the strength of its conformity to the contemporary religious and philosophical climate that Christianity made headway, but in the face of opposition and misunderstanding. Paul declared, "We preach Christ crucified, a stumbling block to the Jews and folly to the Gentiles."[3] After an apparent failure at Athens where Paul expounded Christianity in terms more acceptable to the philosophers of the day, the apostle resolved to make his evangelical appeal in Corinth "not in plausible words of wisdom, but in demonstration of the Spirit and power."[4]

The victory of the Christian message owed little to its inherent plausibility. In fact, in Athens the doctrine of the resurrection was judged wholly *implausible* by the thinking elite. A whole century would go by before Justin Martyr wrote his learned apology of Christianity addressed to the Emperor Antonius Pius. And long after Paul, the Platonists, Celsus (c. 177) and Porphiry (233 - 304), would be making their attempts to discredit Christianity on strictly rational terms. Efforts to show affinities between Stoic and Christian ethics, or between Platonic and Christian transcendentalism, or Philo's doctrine of the Logos and the Logos of the Gospel of John can never produce evidence that these affinities were anything more than latent, or that those better qualified to judge were aware of these affinities and thereby predisposed favorably to the Christian message. Those in the apostolic circle who were in better position to evaluate such affinities simply ignored them, stressing on every occasion the antagonisms rather than the similarities. In Paul's estimate not many "wise according to worldly standards"[5] accepted the Christian message; it would be safe to say that those who did accept did so not because of the philosophical plausibility of the gospel but in spite of its implausibility.

In the pagan world Christianity faced not only philosophical opposition and ridicule but also mounting political and religious pressure. Typical of this was emperor worship, which became fashionable after Domitian's insistence on being recognized as *dominus ac deus* ("lord and god"). Originated in the province of Asia, where a temple to *diva Roma* ("goddess of Rome") and Augustus had been erected as early as 29 B.C., emperor worship gradually extended to the West. Deification was decreed for Julius Caesar by the senate in 42 B.C., and later it became customary for that body to deify the "good" emperors after their deaths. By contrast, in the East, ever since Alexander had accepted the convenient fiction of posing as the son of Amon, with pharaonic precedent, many of the Hellenistic kings perpetuated the practice of self-deification for political reasons. Domitian (51 - 96), under the spell of Oriental influences combined with a theocratic conception of the state, made claims which were offensive to ancient Roman common sense and totally unacceptable to Christians.

Both their refusal to worship the emperor and their otherworldliness made Christians appear indifferent or hostile to the Roman state. Since public life was interwoven with heathen ritual, Christians felt compelled to withdraw from it. Though ever submissive to the authorities in matters purely secular and willing to render to Caesar the things which belonged to Caesar, their relation to the state could only be negative as long as the state remained thoroughly pagan. "Nothing," Tertullian acknowledged with candor, "is more foreign to us than public affairs." Because of religious implications Christians avoided military service and public offices. And the very universalism of the Christian community, in which Romans and barbarians were brothers in Christ, was enough to stigmatize it in the eyes of Roman patriots as being anti-Roman. "Was the emperor's birthday celebrated, the houses of the Christians remained dark in the illuminated cities, and their doors were not garlanded. Were games given in honor of some triumph, no Christian allowed himself to be seen in the circus, or in the amphitheater. To strew incense to the emperor, to do homage to the image of the emperor, to swear by his genius, was accounted by the Christians a fall into idolatry."[6]

In view of this apparent aloofness, Christians were deemed guilty of high treason. Whereas to a patriot the eternal duration of Rome was a cherished dogma, the Christians expected the speedy destruction of the whole world, including Rome, and rejoiced in this expectation as the sign of their redemption. To the heathen a totalitarian state, whose demands invaded every area of life and whose laws were regarded no less than divine, presented no problem. He might flout those demands in practice, but he would not object to them on grounds of conscience. Not so the Christian. He would pray for the welfare of the emperor and the prosperity of the state, but to call the emperor *Dominus* was a betrayal of the faith, because to him Christ alone was Lord. From this constant antagonism arose the repeated cry against Christians, *Non licit esse vos,* "It is not lawful for you to exist."

Though no general and systematic effort to suppress Christianity was made until Decius (249 - 251), persecution flared sporadically under Domitian and under some of the more conscientious emperors such as Trajan, Hadrian, and Marcus Aurelius. They perceived, however dimly, that the existence of the Roman state was threatened by the new spirit of Christianity. A totalitarian state could not well coexist with a religion which placed such a high premium on the freedom of conscience. For the individual the test of loyalty, as one would expect, would focus on the issue of emperor worship. The following is a typical case, among thousands, of the trial of a Christian before a Roman authority:

"Proconsul: 'You ought to love our princes as behooves a man who lives under the laws of the Roman Empire.'

"Achatius: 'By whom is the emperor more loved than by the Christians? We supplicate for him unceasingly a long life, a just government of his peoples, a peaceful reign, prosperity for the army and the whole world.'

"Proconsul: 'Good, but in order to prove your obedience, sacrifice with us to his honor.'

"Achatius: 'I pray to God for my emperor, but a sacrifice neither he should require nor we pay. Who may offer divine honor to a man?' "[7]

Upon this declaration he was sentenced to death.

For Christianity the world unrolled no red carpet. Deep-seated and irreconcilable antagonisms made its acceptance by the pagan world, at least by its officialdom and intelligentsia, practically impossible. Those who embraced it did so at the risk of their lives and of every worldly prospect. Nevertheless, quietly and irresistibly, as leaven working in a lump of dough, it eventually gained the allegiance of millions, a triumph of faith contrary to every human expectation.

Christianity's closest competitor for the allegiance of the masses of the empire in the third century was Mithraism, which resembled it in many respects. Mithraism had numerous affinities with the other mystery cults. Its concept of *Sol Invictus* enjoyed great popular appeal. It revived the *taurobolium,* or baptism with the blood of a bull, to which regenerative virtue was ascribed. Its votaries faced no persecution, were not conscience-bound to clash with emperor worship or state loyalty. Mithraism enjoyed imperial patronage under Aurelian (270 - 275), and later under Julian the Apostate (361 - 363). F. Cumont asserts that "Mithraism reached the apogee of its power toward the middle of the third century, and it appeared for a moment as if the world were on the verge of becoming Mithraic."[8] But it failed. Observers of the historical scene in the third century would never guess that in the unequal contest, as far as objective evidence goes, Mithraism in the West would go down into oblivion in a few generations, and Christianity would survive both it and the empire.

Mithraism votary receives baptism of bull's blood. During the third century Mithraism became Christianity's closest competitor. Restoration from the taurobolic altar found at Fourvieres in 1704. Historical Pictures Service, Chicago.

The "reasons" commonly alleged for the success of Christianity would apply even better to Mithraism. It catered to the religious aspirations of the age, promised regeneration and eternal life, supported a sound morality, appealed to mysticism, was popular with the army, and enjoyed imperial favor. Nevertheless, whereas Christianity went forth "conquering and to conquer," Mithraism dissipated into nothingness.

In his celebrated history Edward Gibbon attributed the success of Christianity to the following "causes": (1) the enthusiasm of the early Christians, (2) their belief in immortality, with future rewards and punishments, (3) miracles, (4) the high ethical code of its first professors, and (5) efficient organization on imperial patterns.[9] But Gibbon fails to explain why a pious fraud—to him Christianity was no more than that—could have infused believers with such all-conquering enthusiasm. Nor does he account why belief in immortality and miracles could be so efficacious in the Christian message while it had no such efficacy in the mystery cults which promoted similar beliefs. Judaism and Stoicism also upheld high ethical standards, and yet they were destitute of vitality and persuasiveness. The truth is that no rationalization which leaves God out of account will ever fully explain the initial success and perennial strength of Christianity.

Lecky showed much greater perspicacity in giving his rationale of the success of Christianity when he wrote: "The chief cause of its success was the congruity of its teaching with the spiritual nature of mankind. It was because it was true to the moral sentiments of the age, because it represented faithfully the supreme type of excellence to which men were then tending, because it corresponded to their religious wants, aims, emotions, because the whole spiritual being could thus expand and expatiate under its influence, that it planted its roots so deeply in the hearts of men."[10]

Lecky underlines the correspondence between Christianity and the religious wants and aims of the times, its conformity to the sentiments of the age. But he cannot explain the reason this new religion from the East, founded by an "obscure Galilean Prophet," supported by a handful of illiterate disciples, and bearing the stigma of a Jewish sect, did in fact present the world with "the supreme type of excellence to which men were then tending." Nothing short of a miracle can explain it. There was indeed a remarkable congruity between the teachings of Christ and "the spiritual nature of mankind." But how could He have discovered it in the unpromising environment of Nazareth, shut off from the crosscurrents of contemporary thought, unless He were in truth the Son of the living God!

The inherent congruity between the message of Jesus and man's spiritual needs was not something that could be argued out. It carried no prima facie evidence that the intellectual elite of the Roman world could recognize. It was too subtle for logical analysis. Yet it was real enough to be felt by the less sophisticated members of society. This attunement between the Christian message and man's need could be apprehended by faith, but to the rational man it was folly. Thus it never ceased to elicit the bitterest acrimony from those unable to explain its irresistible appeal.

Christianity, wherever preached in the empire, evoked either the most loving devotion or the deepest hatred. Man could not stand indifferent to its innate charm. Celsus, who in the time of Marcus Aurelius penned the oldest polemical writing against Christianity, mixed his incisive logic with the vilest invective: "The demon [of the Christians] is not only reviled, but banished from every land and sea, and those who like images are consecrated to him are bound and led to punishment and impaled, whilst the demon—or, as you call him, the Son of God—takes no vengeance on the evildoer."[11]

Celsus cannot be dismissed as an isolated case of blind prejudice. The emperor-philosopher Marcus Aurelius, easily the most conscientious of the Roman rulers, faithful adherent and exponent of the Stoic philosophy, showed nothing but scorn for Christianity. If anyone was qualified by training and position to judge the merits of the new religion and its essential congruity with the aspirations and sentiments of the age, that one should have been the suave Marcus Aurelius, who found time in the midst of the turmoils of the campaign against the Marcomani to write his *Meditations*. But Justin's defense of the faith addressed to the emperor fell upon deaf ears. Both Polycarp and Justin suffered martyrdom under Marcus Aurelius, who went far beyond Trajan by decreeing that the property of the Christians be given to their accusers as an incentive to ignoble denunciation. When persecution raged in Lyons (France), on being consulted, the emperor commanded that convicted Roman Christians be beheaded and the other Christians thrown to the wild beasts.

From the evidence it is clear that Marcus Aurelius was more aware of the ineluctable contradictions between the Christian gospel and the Roman world view than he was of any inherent congruities between it and Stoic philosophy, or "the spiritual nature of mankind."

Looking across the span of the centuries, it is easy to rationalize the triumph of Christianity in terms of its correspondence with the religious needs and aspirations of the age. But realizing that as late as the time of Constantine only one citizen in ten was a Christian, it must be conceded that to the vast majority of the pagan population the new faith presented little attraction. It contradicted convictions made venerable by age, demanded too much self-denial, outraged the carnal mind. Christianity was too uncompromising, too exclusivist, too otherworldly to suit the natural man. Christianity if it were to triumph at all must do it against its environment, on the strength of its divine origin —not because of being favored by circumstances above competitors.

Facing the hostility of pagan lands, Christianity received an even more hostile reception in its own native land. The Gospels leave no doubt that the Jewish hierarchy showed no sympathy to the Galilean Prophet or His disciples. They dogged His path at every step. His Jeremianic stress on religion as a matter of the heart contradicted the legalism so deeply ingrained in the soul of the nation. His unconcern for the traditions of the elders antagonized the Pharisaic party bent on safeguarding the law with man-made regulations. Admittedly the common people sensed that a new prophet had risen, for the thrust of Jesus' preaching was felt as that of Jeremiah or "one of the prophets." But to the authorities Jesus' Messianic claim was preposterous. His role as the Messiah did not meet their expectations. Had He come as a revolutionary to break the yoke of Roman oppression and to establish an earthly kingdom in Davidic style, they might have lent Him their support. But Jesus showed no inclination to accept an earthly crown. In fact, after the miracle of the multiplication of bread He stopped dead in its tracks a popular movement to crown Him king.[12]

Not only did the religious leaders of the nation reject Him, even the common people deserted Him. Putting their loyalty to the test, Jesus preached His "hard" sermon in the synagogue at Capernaum.

"After this many of His disciples drew back and no longer went about with Him."[13] The initial interest in Christ's mission, aroused by the preaching of John the Baptist, turned gradually into indifference, later into blind antagonism, and finally into bitter hatred which could be assuaged by nothing short of His death.

His motives were misinterpreted, His words distorted, His miracles discredited, and His reputation besmudged for the avowed purpose of frustrating His mission. The religious hierarchy correctly reasoned that their position was threatened by Christ's teaching on the kingdom of God. Should He be right, then their lifeless literalism, their legalistic insistence, their mundane ambitions would be swept away as by a divine wind. Since they could not allow this to happen, the cross stands as a monument to man's self-exaltation and hatred and the magnitude of Christ's self-abasement and love.

This brings us to the most perplexing paradox in history. It is customary to expatiate upon the long-drawn-out and painstaking preparation, involving to greater or lesser degree all mankind, to ready the stage for the divine disclosure in "the fullness of time." This *praeparatio evangelica,* the preparation of the world for the gospel of Christ, is the clue to the travails of the human soul in all the centuries that preceded the advent of Christ. It puts convincing meaning into mankind's slow pilgrimage toward a clearer understanding of God's redemptive purpose. It sets in proper perspective Egypt's millennial hope of immortality; Babylon's concept of cosmic order; Zoroaster's understanding of the moral struggle between good and evil, light and darkness, issuing into a final judgment and the triumph of good; Hella's contribution to logical thought; the mystery religions' spiritual premonitions; and, above all, Israel's mission as a people chosen to illumine the Gentiles with the bright light of divine revelation. Undeniably this view of the pre-Christian past, clearly grasped by Paul and later expanded by Eusebius of Caesarea in his *Ecclesiastical History,* introduces meaning into history as no rival view ever did. So radical is this view of history that it stands or falls with the divine claims of Christianity itself.

And yet when Christ came, the world did not greet Him as the fulfillment of man's millennial hope. Very few were aware that divinity had broken into history. Herein lies the paradox. It seemed as if the travail of the centuries had been in vain. *Koinē* Greek had become the universal language, but that was not the language in which Christ would preach. The world was united as never before under the aegis of the Roman Empire, but the Jewish nation chafed under Roman control. Unprecedented prosperity and security were enjoyed far and wide under the *Pax Romana,* but Christ was nailed to a cross, and His disciples were later persecuted as disturbers of the peace. Hellenistic syncretism had habituated people to religious amalgamation and eclecticism, but true Christianity resisted all attempts at compromise with current religious thought. The breakdown of the city-state political system fostered rank individualism in place of collective security, as did the appearance of energetic leaders such as Alexander; but Christ preached self-denial as a check against self-assertiveness. In an age of men bent on self-seeking and worldly success, Christ insisted that "whoever would save his life will lose it; and whoever loses his life for My sake and the gospel's will save it."[14]

The paradox is summed up in this fact: While Christ was rightfully expected "to bring peace on earth," yet He Himself stated that He did "not come to bring peace, but a sword."[15] Christ offered no easy clue to resolve the tension between popular Messianic expectation and the fulfillment. It was not that the tension consisted in man's entertaining too high hopes which overshot the fulfillment, but that man cherished hopes too mundane to come to grips with man's transcendental destiny; his comprehension of the divine goal in history could not be attained by sheer logic, but could only be apprehended by faith. Thus, while to the sophisticated minds of the day the news of world redemption achieved through the death and resurrection of Christ sounded like folly, to those endowed with faith, capable of spiritual discernment, the "word of the cross" was indeed "the power of God."[16]

Yet what could be discerned by the believer was not truth on some esoteric, unhistorical plane, but realities which had transpired on the historical level and had been attested by reliable witnesses—realities just as verifiable as the fact that Tiberius Caesar began to rule in A.D. 14. Christ's first advent was no less a historical event than the procuratorship of Pilate, but its eternal significance was not self-evident to the "natural" man. Once his faith had been aroused by the preaching of the gospel under the unction of the Holy Spirit, then the significance of the cross became plain to him as something eternally true. To those oblivious to the claims of the gospel the story of the cross remained a "scandal." As Alan Richardson puts it: "This is the 'scandal' of the Biblical witness, as it is the scandal of the incarnation: that the Eternal should have become historical and that, therefore, the historical should have become the bearer of the eternal Word. The historical Jesus who is the eternal Word is part of the history of our world. The Word became flesh. The factuality of God's action in the events to which the Bible testifies is . . . the historic Christian faith."[17]

Thus from the Biblical view all history prior to the advent of Christ was indeed a preparation for that event. The eternal Word could not become flesh any earlier than it did. Changes in the social, political, philosophical, and religious order had to take place so that when the seed of the gospel should be sown it would not merely fall on rocky ground. Jesus had, according to Mark, inaugurated His ministry in Galilee with the startling message, "The time is fulfilled."[18] Time had been irreversibly moving toward the divine disclosure in Christ.

Yet the generation that saw and heard Christ was no more capable of discerning the "signs of the times" than an observer is aware of movement by casting a casual glance at the pointers of a clock. They lacked a sense of perspective which could be gained only by a quickened awareness of man's historical past. The world had changed considerably in the course of the centuries, but to the casual onlooker "all things" had "continued as they were from the beginning of creation."[19] Mankind was just as oblivious of movement in history then as we are of the motion of our planet on its orbit around the sun. Both are matters of fact, and yet imperceptible to the senses. But whereas man may be convinced of the earth's orbital motion by scientific reasoning, of God's movement in history climaxing in the Christ-event he can only be persuaded by faith.

REFERENCES

1. R. G. Collingwood, *The Idea of History,* page 178.
2. John 1:11, KJV.
3. 1 Corinthians 1:23.
4. 1 Corinthians 2:4.
5. 1 Corinthians 1:26.
6. G. Uhlhorn, *Conflict of Christianity With Heathenism,* tr., pages 231, 232.
7. Smith and Wace, *Dictionary of Christian Biography,* Vol. 1, p. 11.

8. F. Cumont, *The Mysteries of Mithra,* page 199.
9. See E. Gibbon, *The Decline and Fall of the Roman Empire,* ch. XV.
10. W. E. H. Lecky, *History of European Morals,* Vol. 1, pp. 388, 389.
11. G. Uhlhorn, *op. cit.,* p. 296.
12. See John 6:15.
13. Verse 66.
14. Mark 8:35.
15. Matthew 10:34.
16. 1 Corinthians 1:18.
17. Alan Richardson, *The Bible in the Age of Science,* page 141.
18. Mark 1:15.
19. 2 Peter 3:4.

Chapter 11

The Time Between

It would be an arbitrary procedure to take Paul's writings as a guide to interpret pre-Christian history, particularly his discourse before the sophisticated Athenians, and yet ignore what he might have to say concerning events still in the future. To believers in divine inspiration what a Biblical writer utters about the future is just as pregnant with meaning as what he says about the past. Of course, if divine inspiration is denied, then a Biblical writer might still be a witness to the past on his own right, and a reflector of views current in his day as to the meaning of history. His testimony would not be devoid of interest, but it would certainly be devoid of that authority which alone would make the study of the Biblical view of history worthwhile.

Heilsgeschichte, the story of redemption, does not stop with Christ's first advent. If, in the words of E. Rust, "the final meaning of history must be a purpose of redemption which is actualized by God in history itself,"[1] then this redemptive purpose, of which the cross is both symbol and pledge, must yet find its consummation. The decisive victory over sin and death has been won at the cross, but the full benefit of this victory has not yet been realized. In the words of Paul, "We ourselves, who have the first fruits of the Spirit, groan inwardly as we wait for adoption as sons, the redemption of our bodies. For in this hope we were saved."[2] Full redemption is much more than a subjective experience affecting only the inner man. It encompasses all of man, all of the earth, including man's historical existence.

Barth's view that Christ's resurrection alone is significant and that, in consequence, the world and its history become meaningless and irrelevant, or, in other words, that the kingdom of God is radically discontinuous with the world,[3] cannot be reconciled with the Biblical view. Obviously Barth's existentialist frame of reference with its obsession for the present moment forbids him to regard past history seriously. This existential insistence on the radical discontinuity between salvific and secular history flies in the face of the incarnation, in which the "Word became flesh" and God tabernacled with man. And if history since the cross is irrelevant, it is hard to see how prior history, particularly the history of Israel leading up to the Christ-event, could be relevant.

The indifference for past history is the recognized hallmark of existentialism. It should surprise no one that for the Bultmannians the factuality of the gospel narrative fades into convenient myths, and to more radical existentialist theologians that it fades into mere symbols.

Typical of the existentialist outlook is Bultmann's answer to the quest for the meaning of history. "The meaning of history lies always in the present, and when the present is conceived as the eschatological present by Christian faith, the meaning in history is realized. Man who complains: 'I cannot see meaning in history and therefore my life, interwoven in history, is meaningless,' is to be admonished: do not look around yourself into universal history, you must look into your own personal history. Always in your present lies the meaning in history, and you cannot see it as a spectator, but only in your responsible decisions. In every moment slumbers the possibility of being the eschatological moment. You must awaken it."[4]

This seems poor consolation to man in his actual plight. Man is aware of his personal history, but he knows too poignantly that his little life cannot confer meaning to universal history. Inversely, however, universal history, if man could discover its meaning, might confer this meaning into his own life. The whole is not explained by the part, but the part by the whole.

We may well agree with Bultmann that man standing within history cannot detect its meaning. But God, who stands outside history and presides over its course, might reveal its meaning to man. And that is precisely what Christians believe He has done. It is not a meaning discoverable by reason, for then man must stand at the end or goal of history and survey history as an accomplished fact. It is rather a meaning apprehended by faith on the basis of a divine revelation.

God has vouchsafed for man not a philosophy of history, but a theology of history. Even then man must not presume to read God's providence in history as an open book. Paul warns against this danger in his letter to the Romans: "O the depth of the riches and wisdom and knowledge of God! How unsearchable are His judgments and how inscrutable His ways!"[5]

With this caveat in mind, we may well ask, What, then, is the meaning of history from the cross to the second advent? Students of the Bible will certainly agree that the *eschaton,* or final event, was not realized in Christ's first advent. The New Testament looks forward to a glorious consummation in the second coming of Christ. Time elapsed since the resurrection of Christ, however prolonged, is an interim in anticipation of a complete redemption, when death will be swallowed up in the resurrection of the last day. One may admit the eschatological nature of the Christ-event in view of the expectations of the Old Testament church. And yet one must draw a distinction between the eschatological age Christ inaugurated and its apocalyptic culmination. This is the last *aeon,* the terminal age; but it, too, will pass away at the *parousia,* the personal advent of Christ. The duration of the last age was no problem to the apostolic church. Few realized at first that a long historical interval might lie ahead until the end of the age. As J. M. Connolly puts it, "It is this mysterious period of 'time between' that constitutes the nub of the problem of history for the Christian."[6]

Attempts to reconstruct the New Testament view of history on the basis of realized eschatology, or the idea that the final event of sacred history, the second coming of Christ, has already occurred, have shattered on the overwhelming evidence that the apostolic church looked forward to translation and glory. It was a church fully aware that its hope in Christ awaited fulfillment. Teachings such as "that the resurrection is past already," were branded as heresy.[7] No mystical union with the resurrected Saviour, however basic in the believer's experience, was ever seen as realizing the hope centered in the visible return of their Lord. In neither Gospels nor Epistles is there any confusion between the subjective, salvific, personal experience of the individual believer and the collective hope of the church to witness Christ's return when He would overcome the sting of death.

The problems which the delay of the *parousia* posed for the primitive church were trying but not insuperable. The possibility that the final consummation of the ages, with the establishment of God's visible kingdom, might not come in their own generation dawned gradually upon the church as a painful realization. But it would be false to say that the concept of redemptive history was an afterthought resulting from the embarrassment over unfulfilled hopes. That a time interval would elapse between Christ's ascension and His return was freely understood. The disappointment was only concerned with the length of this interval. The church was always aware that there was a task to be accomplished on earth in the intervening time. The delay introduced no radical departure from the belief that the task of acquainting men everywhere with the decisive event of the cross must first be accomplished.

Echoes of disappointed hopes may be overheard in some of the last New Testament writings. Questions such as, "Where is the promise of His coming?"[8] must have been raised ever more frequently as the decades stretched into centuries. The answer to such skeptical queries took three basic formulations.

First, "With the Lord one day is as a thousand years, and a thousand years as one day."[9] The implication was that God's time scale was radically different from man's, and that any complaint about delay was groundless, since man's reckoning of time was not the same as God's. The believer must be prepared to accept the fact, however disappointing to him, that only in God's own good time would the divine promises be fulfilled.

Second, any apparent delay was bound with God's forbearance, "not wishing that any should perish, but that all should reach repentance."[10] Should the believer begrudge divine forbearance? Should he not rather rejoice that divine mercy did prolong the time of salvation? To insist otherwise would betray callous indifference to those outside the kingdom. If delay as a result of divine forbearance should result in a greater number of saved, that would be additional reason for rejoicing.

The third argument in this pericope lays stress on the element of surprise surrounding "the day of the Lord."[11] The delay, far from generating complacency, should fire believers with eager expectation.

Since the apocalyptic end-event would mock at every human timetable, then the only proper attitude for a Christian would be to watch and pray, for no one knows "when the time will come."[12] The quintessence of nonchalant complacency is portrayed in the attitude of the "wicked servant" who said to himself, "my master is delayed," and went about in riotous indulgence.[13]

That such attitude of expectancy persisted into the subapostolic age is evident from the early patristic literature. But early believers would have been more than human if the original sense of urgency and expectation had not worn away with the passing of time and the gradual accommodation of the church to the world. A revival of the belief that the end of the age was close at hand was fostered by Montanism in the late second century. The new chiliastic, or millennial, hopes of the Montanists promoted a reaction against the secular tendencies which increasingly pervaded the church. Unfortunately, as is so often the case, a fanatical streak marred this Montanist witness to the advent hope and blunted its effectiveness. Even so Montanism, with its ascetic ideals opposed to contemporary laxity, captured the loyalty of as great a thinker as Tertullian (c. 150 - 225).

In the course of time it was inevitable that the church, which had begun as the transient fellowship of the saints who shared in the "blessed hope," should assume increasing significance as a permanent institution. As generation after generation of believers passed off the stage, the church as "the body of Christ" was the one enduring entity to survive the ravages of time. If the original congregations scattered from Jerusalem to Rome thought of themselves as interim fellowships, soon to be absorbed into the coming kingdom and therefore in no need of complex organization, they must have become gradually aware that more was implied in Christ's sayings concerning the church than they had at first realized.

Through the church, more than through any individual, was "the manifold wisdom of God" to "be made known to the principalities and powers in the heavenly places." And this was "according to the eternal purpose" which God had "realized in Christ Jesus our Lord."[14] In a supernal way the church must become "a spectacle to the world, to angels and to men,"[15] a living, enduring demonstration of God's redemptive purpose. The saving work inaugurated by Christ's death

Christ's second coming. As the decades stretched into centuries, this hope was never abandoned. Woodcut by anonymous artist appeared in Luther's first complete Bible. Reproduced in *Woodcuts to the Apocalypse in Dürer's Time,* compiled by Kenneth A. Strand.

and resurrection must be carried to completion through the corporate body of believers, supernaturally endowed with the gifts of the Spirit. In fact, it became evident that God intended that the benefits of the cross be made effective in individual experience through the instrumentality of the church.

In a very profound sense the church thus became an extension of the incarnation. Its historical existence was justified. The time between the first and second advents of Christ was the period given for the church to complete its divine commission of reconciling man to God. "Occupy till I come,"[16] was the watchword given to the church. There was a world to be evangelized, and the return could not take place until this stupendous mission had been fulfilled. As O. Cullmann puts it: "This missionary proclamation of the Church, its preaching of the gospel, gives to the period between Christ's resurrection and *Parousia* its meaning for redemptive history; and it has this meaning through its connection with Christ's present Lordship."[17]

In view of this inescapable fact, if a divine goal is to be found in any area of history, it must be found in the life and mission of the church. It follows that the rationale of all history should be illumined by ecclesiastical history and not vice versa. Some claim to see no evidence of God's providential activity in either profane or sacred history. As a matter of fact, the majority of the Roman world were unaware that events of transcendent importance were transpiring in Palestine in the days of Tiberius. No contemporary secular historian recognized in the transactions of Christ's life and death a turning point of ultimate relevance in world history. Their utter inability to read the signs of the times is typical of men immersed in the historical continuum. Man's very involvement in the historical process deprives him of that sense of perspective without which no value judgments are possible. But if myopia in observers of the contemporary scene is excusable as a natural consequence of man's finitude, no such extenuating circumstance may be invoked by those who have a clear view of two millennia of history.

It would seem reasonable to infer that the failure to see a divine meaning in history is the result of searching for it first in secular rather than in church history. One might say that divine attention focuses in the church and that, therefore, it is in the church that the divine intention in history is to be discerned, if at all. We cannot agree with Karl Löwith, to whom "the will of God" is "a transcendent principle" that "can never become the subject of systematic interpretation . . . even in the history of the church."[18] Löwith thus makes the Christian understanding of history solely "a concern of faith."[19] If the church is the agency through which God reconciles man to Himself, then its history must convey even to secular man a divine meaning, however dimly discerned.

As the time before the expected *parousia* stretched into centuries, the original witnesses of God's mighty revelation in the Christ-event one by one followed the way of all flesh, but the collective witness of the church endowed with the Holy Spirit defied time and persecution. What began as a loosely organized group led by local elders and deacons, whose office was that of temporary shepherds of the flock, whose authority was charismatic, whose Christian commitment was unquestionable, gradually, by imperceptible steps, evolved into a rigid ecclesiastical structure controlled by a self-conscious hierarchy. A precedent for the organization of Christian fellowships existed in the Jewish synagogues scattered through the empire, and possibly in the Essene communities in Palestine. As centers of worship and sources of mutual inspiration, they spearheaded missionary activities aiming at the conversion of their Gentile neighbors. From their united support depended missionaries to surrounding communities. For over two centuries they were no more than propaganda cells, meeting in private houses, rallying points for harassed believers. The Christian churches, in fact, did not attain legal status until Gallienus (A.D. 259 - 268) allowed the Christian faith as *religio licita,* a legal religion. This arrangement was repudiated by the tetrarchy under Diocletian and was only reinstated when Constantine and Licinius issued the Edict of Milan in 313 granting full freedom to Christianity.

Long before Constantine, though, the church was experiencing a radical transformation which can best be characterized as a "fall." Of this *apostasia* Paul had written in his second letter to the Thessalonians, one of the earliest from his pen: "Let no one deceive you in any way; for that day will not come, unless the rebellion comes first, and the man of lawlessness is revealed, the son of perdition, who opposes and exalts himself against every so-called god or object of worship, so that he takes his seat in the temple of God, proclaiming himself to be God. Do you not remember that when I was still with you I told you this? And you know what is restraining him now so that he may be revealed in his time. For the mystery of lawlessness is already at work; only he who now restrains it will do so until he is out of the way. And then the lawless one will be revealed, and the Lord Jesus will slay him with the breath of His mouth and destroy him by His appearing and His coming. The coming of the lawless one by the activity of Satan will be with all power and with pretended signs and wonders, and with all wicked deception for those who are to perish, because they refused to love the truth and so be saved. Therefore God sends upon them a strong delusion, to make them believe what is false, so that all may be condemned who did not believe the truth but had pleasure in unrighteousness."[20]

Whatever obscurities may attach to this apocalyptic passage, this much is clear: a defection would occur affecting the very heart of the church, and this defection would be the result of self-exaltation. Somehow this apostasy would involve a departure from the faith as result of refusal "to love the truth and so be saved." The church, and not only the world, would become the arena of a conflict of cosmic proportions between Christ and the powers of darkness. This controversy which is reenacted over and again in the microcosm of every human existence since Adam's fall, would be projected in large scale into the life of the church itself. Its witness for Christ, far from remaining unequivocal, would be tarnished. The commitment of the church to its Head, Christ, would become ambiguous, its loyalty divided, its gradual secularization a painful reality.

As might be expected, the self-consciousness of the church as the defender of the faith, the custodian of truth, and the channel of divine grace grew with the passing of time. The adjective "catholic" first used by Ignatius originally meant nothing more than universal, but in the strife of heretical controversies it took the added connotation of orthodox. Faced with the challenges of Gnosticism and Montanism, champions of orthodoxy such as Irenaeus appealed to the testimony of those churches which not only had been founded by the apostles, but in which the apostolic teaching had been preserved by an orderly succession of bishops. The simple baptismal confession of the apostolic age, "Jesus is Lord,"[21] was expanded until by the time of Hippolytus (170? - 235) in Rome it also included belief in "the Holy Church." This trend found fullest expression in the teachings of Cyprian from the middle of the third century. "There is no salvation out of the church," he asserted. And again: "He can no longer have God for his Father, who has not the church for his mother."[22]

The growing self-consciousness fanned by religious controversies was on the other hand tempered and subdued by the recurring persecutions which flared up in the middle of the third century under the emperors Decius and Valerian. In fact, the overt success of the church in winning converts combined with its closely knit hierarchical organization, could not but inspire the odium and suspicion of the Roman Empire in its struggle for survival in the face of mounting barbarian pressure on the frontiers, and internal economic and political decay. But the persecution unleashed by Diocletian and Galerius which raged for a few years (303 - 311) and caused untold suffering and the destruction of much property, was less baneful in its effects upon the church than the climate of toleration and eventual official support under Constantine and his successors. "In winning its freedom from its enemies," says church historian Williston Walker, "it [the church] had come largely under the control of the occupant of the Roman imperial throne. A fateful union with the state had begun."[23]

Eusebius of Caesarea, the father of church historians, goes so far as to recognize in the Diocletian persecution a divine judgment upon a church growing corrupt in a climate of ease and prosperity. "Increasing freedom," he says, "transformed our character to arrogance and sloth; we began envying and abusing each other, cutting our own throats, as occasion offered, with weapons of sharp-edged words; rulers hurled themselves at rulers and laymen waged party fights against laymen, and unspeakable hypocrisy and dissimulation were carried to the limit of wickedness. . . . Those of us who were supposed to be pastors cast off the restraining influence of the Spirit of God and quarreled heatedly with each other, engaged solely in swelling the disputes, threats, envy, and mutual hostility and hate, frantically demanding the despotic power they coveted."[24]

Kenneth S. Latourette faces the problem of the apostasy of the church with greater frankness than most church historians. He writes:

"Indeed, it is a question whether any visible institution, especially if it becomes large, can avoid falling victim in part to trends in the direction of the power which crucified Jesus.

"The danger to Christianity was augmented when the state made its peace with the church. Until then . . . Christians tended to keep aloof from government and many, perhaps the majority of the Christians, believed that loyalty to Christ was inconsistent with holding civil or military office. . . . Beginning with Constantine, that attitude was weakened. The emperors and an increasing proportion of the officials and of the troops assumed the Christian name. . . . Emperors exercised their power to interfere in the affairs of the church. . . .

"It is clear that the church was the product of the gospel. It is also clear that the visible, institutionalized church, whether Catholic or one of the bodies which dissented, was shot through and through with contradictions to the gospel. As Augustine frankly admitted, the two cities, the earthly and the heavenly, are intermingled."[25]

Commenting on the fifth-century controversy over Mary as *Theotokos,* which shook the Eastern churches and resulted in the banishment of Nestorius, G. Heard writes: "Yet it is clear that Christianity had no longer the support it once had from the masses. The church had ceased to be what it had been in Clement's day—a wonderful demonstration that the myth had become historical, the promise actual, the hope fulfilled. Only imposition by military Byzantine force was now able to make the greater part of the Levant accept the particular 'party line' imposed by Constantinople."[26]

The church of the early fourth century bore as little resemblance to the apostolic church as Roman institutions under Diocletian bore to those under Augustus. The growing self-consciousness of the church fed on prestige which could only increase as Rome declined and as the cross receded into the dim past. By choosing to make the church the channel of His saving grace, its Founder assumed the liability inherent in man's freedom. Such risks recall the risks God encountered in bringing free moral agents into existence in the first place. The possibility of pride and self-assertiveness was inherent in both situations. To preclude sin and fall would have meant to bar human freedom.

Just as man, the church bears God's image; and just as man, the church is liable to fall. The church is a divine institution and yet composed of men subject to sin. As a divinely ordained institution, of which Pentecost is a reminder, it must ultimately fulfill its redemptive mission in the world. Composed as it is of fallible human beings, it might at times betray its mission and disappoint its Author. Meant by its divine Founder to go out "conquering and to conquer,"[27] making ever wider the circle of Christ's kingdom, it might, nevertheless, by its conformity to the world, delay the attainment of this goal. The church did in fact lose its "first love," and fell indeed from its original level of dedication and purity.[28] It is conceivable that had the church remained faithful to its "first love" and carried with the original impetus the good news of the Christ-event to the world, long since "the kingdom of the world" would have "become the kingdom of our Lord and of His Christ."[29] That this was no idle dream even in the fourth century is demonstrated by the ability of Christianity to win tribe after tribe of the oak-worshiping barbarians in central Europe, and under the Nestorian drive to push its conquest of the civilized East right through to the Yellow Sea.

From this it follows that secular history might have coalesced with sacred history long since. The inner circle, the church, of which Christ is the center, to use Cullmann's imagery, would have leavened and transformed the outer circle of the world, and Christ would reign supreme. Delay, though, does not mean defeat. In this spiritual warfare, the decisive battle was fought and won on the cross. What remains, however long the centuries may roll, are only mopping-up operations. In the interim until the *parousia,* secular history goes on. The role of any theology of history is to discover where the two histories, that of the church and that of the world, have interacted, and whether one or both bear the evidence of providential guidance.

First it should be clear that belief in the providential guidance of the historical Christian church is not inconsistent with the belief that the church has experienced a fall. Its departure from the original gospel is plain enough for all to see. Each step of the apostasy can be well documented. Like the believers in Galatia, the church was "running well" to start with.[30] But like the Galatians, it did not persevere in obedience to the truth. It defected to another gospel. It became legalistic and sacramentarian. It conformed to the world instead of transforming the world. It became rich and complacent. But unlike the fall of the Roman Empire, the fall of the church was not final. Secular institutions wear out and must be replaced. Their collapse is irrevocable. Made obsolete by changing conditions, they must be discarded. Not so with the body of the living Christ, the church. Its witness may become garbled at times, but never forever silenced. Its luster may be dimmed by human frailty and sin, and yet God's redeeming grace is at work in it to renew it. The church by its recalcitrance may delay the realization of its hope, but not permanently thwart it.

The demand for evidence that the church has been providentially led in the fulfillment of its mission in history is not rooted in lack of faith, but in the conviction that the God who acted redemptively in the history of Israel, and who brought the church into existence in order to make known to the world the unsurpassable riches of His grace, would not cease to give evidence of His concern for its ultimate success. If its mission is to be realized not in a purely subjective sense but in objective time, then it should be possible to verify its achievements on the historical plane.

Granted that spiritual realities must be spiritually discerned, and that the points where the suprahistorical touches the historical are not occurrences open to ordinary historical rules of evidence, it would even so be incredible that the most sublime task in which the Deity is engaged, the redemption of mankind, would not make so much as a ripple on the earthly scene. Granted also that in his earthly pilgrimage man must walk by faith and not by sight as part of the spiritual discipline to which he has been made subject as result of sin, it would yet be reasonable to expect that a loving Father would vouchsafe for man some glimpses of His benevolent providence. Such intimations, assuring man of meaning in history, would not be a substitute for faith, but an aid to it.

Were it not for heresies and theological controversies, reformation and counterreformation, the history of the church would be extremely short. A victorious, sinless church would abridge both its history and that of the world. As remarked before, both histories would long since have coalesced into sacred history. But this calls for no surprise. Were it not for the tragedy of sin, the first two chapters of Genesis would be joined to the last two of Revelation, and there would be no intervening history. The bulk of the Scriptures is made up of the history of man's failures and God's redemptive acts culminating in the cross. Likewise the bulk of history, both ecclesiastical and profane, is composed mostly of the recital of man's foibles and egotism, interspersed with a few tableaux of truly noble and unselfish deeds.

Even though tragic, man's history is not "an idiot's tale full of sound and fury." From the Biblical viewpoint history does carry a meaning. It could not be otherwise in a world which is the object of God's love and concern.

Yet to affirm this does not imply that the believer can fit every minor and major event into a coherent whole. Faith in a divine providence does not necessarily confer on him the gift of prophetic interpretation. In fact, most believers are content to say that the whole of history will eventually reveal a meaning, and that for the time being we see more often than not "only puzzling reflections in a mirror."[31] In what sense, then, is the believer's position better than that of the unbeliever? In the sense that he rests assured that history moves toward a goal of God's own choice, and that this goal is no other than to "reconcile to Himself all things" through Christ, "whether on earth or in heaven."[32]

The apostasy of the church occupies a key position in any Christian view of history. It would be difficult indeed to justify the presence of a perfect church, loyal to its mission of evangelizing the world, not having completed its task after almost two millennia. But strangely enough, O. Cullmann and others who have sketched theologies of history gloss over the fall of the church and, as a result, their attempt at finding meaning in contemporary history acquires an aura of incredibility.

At best their view of history is static and fails to come to grips with real issues. It conveys to the reader the false impression that nothing significant occurred since the central redemptive event of Christ's passion, death, and resurrection. The church is introduced as the mystical body of Christ, an extension of the incarnation, erected, as it were, upon a pedestal of untouchability, and there left in beatific contemplation while the stream of history rolls by. The interim history between the cross and the *parousia* is dismissed with a few condescending remarks. Only the end points in the line of time have significance.

On the other hand, for the neoorthodox there are no points of contact between the history of God's saving grace for men and the history of men's deeds, since the first is transferred to a timeless realm. It belongs to another dimension of existence. In consequence, either because redemptive history is conceived statically as a line between two points, or because it is projected to another plane where time does not count, the Christian theologian has nothing to say about mundane history, which is the one clamoring for interpretation.

Conceived as a purely divine institution, the church has no history and can cast no light upon secular history. But once its divine-human nature is conceded, it enters the stream of history and may illumine all of history. It is a divine institution because its founder is the Lord Jesus Christ, who, even though one with God, entered human history in the incarnation. Its life as an ongoing institution is sustained by the indwelling presence of the Holy Spirit. And yet the church is also human, because its members belong to the human family. The fact that the Christian in the act of conversion is adopted into the family of God does not make him less human. His finitude as creature and his liability to sin are not changed. As long as he lives, the tension between the heavenly call and the earthly bent of his nature continues to exist.

Likewise the church does not cease to be human because it is the body of Christ, or the temple of God, to use some of the several metaphors employed by New Testament writers. The body of the individual member is also called "the temple of the living God,"[33] and yet it is obviously true that the individual believer, in spite of his exalted calling, experiences sin and fall. A cursory reading of the letters to the Corinthians and to the Galatians makes one painfully aware that not only individuals, but whole congregations, even considerable segments of the church, experienced partial or total apostasy. The letters of Revelation 2 and 3 are believed to describe typical conditions in real churches at the end of the apostolic age. They portray a falling away from the first love (Ephesus), the harboring of heresies (Pergamum and Thyatira), imperfect works (Sardis), lukewarm complacency (Laodicea). It is a picture far from flattering, but true to life.

Thus seen, these churches appear less holy, but more credible. If these churches are representative—and it must be admitted that they are—then the question whether the church could experience a fall becomes purely academic. The very presence of the church in the world today is evidence that after two millennia it has not completed its divine mission. Contrast this fact with Paul's jubilant tone as he sees Christian congregations mushrooming throughout the *oikoumenē*. In one letter he writes, "The gospel which has come to you, as indeed in the whole world it is bearing fruit and growing."[34] To him it looked as if the consummation of the age might lie in the not-too-distant future, since the fulfillment of the foremost sign of the end—"This gospel of the kingdom will be preached throughout the whole world, as a testimony to all nations"[35]—loomed to him as a distinct possibility.

That the end did not come must be ascribed not to God's failure to fulfill His promise but to the dereliction of the church. The objection that God's sovereignty is jeopardized by making His redemptive purpose in any way dependent upon man's response and cooperation is irrelevant. No theological legerdemain can obviate the fact that God entrusted the church with a task. The parables of the talents and of the pounds, in both of which the main thrust is on a continuing work during waiting periods,[36] make it clear that man is charged with a responsibility in the fulfillment of the divine plan. In both parables failure to meet the responsibility entailed punishment. Punishment is morally right where failure occurs in freedom. God's sovereignty is nowhere infringed because He chooses to share with His church the responsibility for calling a lost world to Himself.

NOTES AND REFERENCES

1. E. Rust, *Towards the Theological Understanding of History,* page 114.
2. Romans 8:23, 24.
3. See J. M. Connolly, *Human History and the Word of God,* page 111.
4. R. Bultmann, *The Presence of Eternity,* page 155.
5. Romans 11:33.
6. J. M. Connolly, *op. cit.,* p. 105.
7. 2 Timothy 2:18.
8. 2 Peter 3:4.
9. 2 Peter 3:8.
10. Verse 9.
11. Verse 10.
12. Mark 13:33.
13. Matthew 24:48-51.
14. Ephesians 3:10, 11.
15. 1 Corinthians 4:9.

16. Luke 19:13, KJV.
17. O. Cullmann, *Christ and Time,* page 157.
18. Karl Löwith, *Meaning in History,* page 193.
19. *Ibid.,* p. 186.
20. 2 Thessalonians 2:3-12. It would be a disservice to the Biblical witness to quote Paul's view of history as contained, for example, in his discourse before the Areopagus, and relegate his writing about a coming apostasy as irrelevant apocalyptic. There is no question among scholars about the Pauline authorship of Second Thessalonians. Unbiased handling of the Scriptural evidence would demand that equal weight be given to Paul's statement concerning the future of the Church, as to any of his theological expositions.
21. 1 Corinthians 12:3.
22. W. Walker, *A History of the Christian Church,* page 70.
23. *Ibid.,* p. 111.
24. Eusebius, *The History of the Church,* Book 8, chapter 1.
25. Kenneth S. Latourette, *A History of Christianity,* page 262.
26. G. Heard, *Is God in History?* page 210.
27. Revelation 6:2. See O. Cullmann, *op. cit.,* pp. 160 ff.
28. Revelation 2:4, 5, KJV.
29. Revelation 11:15.
30. Galatians 5:7.
31. 1 Corinthians 13:12, NEB.
32. Colossians 1:20.
33. 1 Corinthians 3:16. Compare 2 Corinthians 6:16. The first applies to the individual believer; the second, to the church.
34. Colossians 1:5, 6.
35. Matthew 24:14.
36. Matthew 25:14-30; Luke 19:12-27.

Chapter 12

The Second Fall

It is the painful but ineluctable duty of the Christian student of history to devote special attention to the dark chapter of the failure of the church, because it alone explains the delay of the next advent and may provide the key to the meaning of secular history. It does not furnish anyone with an aprioristic pattern of future events, since man's response to divine and human confrontations remains a response in freedom. For this reason, what the next turn in history shall be will elude human guess. But the admission that the church did fail and come short of the divine expectation may well give us an a posteriori insight into the significance of major trends in history. It is urgent, therefore, to analyze in more detail the nature of this failure of the church.

This failure of the church affected not only its periphery, some scattered members or congregations here and there, but also its very heart. On the other hand, its failure may not be conceived as of the nature of Adam's fall, the result of one pivotal decision of irrevocable consequences. It must rather be diagnosed as a gradual sickness extending over decades and centuries, moving from the center to the periphery, eventually poisoning every cell of the body. It was not the result of any one decision, either on the part of an individual however prominent, a congregation, or a church council. As the pages of the New Testament make transparently clear, individuals and congregations failed and were restored over and again.

Neither was it the result of some inner necessity or a deficiency of divine grace. Endowed with the Holy Spirit, the church was fully equal to its task. In fact, its initial impetus, going out "conquering and to conquer," was fully worthy of its divine Mover. The impact the original proclamation of the gospel made could only be described as turning "the world upside down."[1] The amazing vitality of the primitive church held the promise that within a generation or two it might evangelize the world. "All authority in heaven and on earth" had been given to its Founder, whose presence within the church was assured "to the close of the age."[2]

Neither may its failure be ascribed to incoercible external circumstances. The chapter "Christianity Against Its Environment" makes this abundantly clear. Social and political pressures against the nascent church only spurred its evangelizing zeal. In a very real sense "the blood of the martyrs was the seed of the church." When persecutions broke out, the church went underground, its courage unabated. The stupendous thing is that the church could actually thrive under persecution. When this gave way to toleration, and later to imperial favor under Constantine and his successors, zeal turned to complacency, humility to pride, reliance upon God to dependence on political power.

The fact is that no "reasons" can be adduced for the failure of the church, if "reasons" mean justifying circumstances. To adduce "reasons" amounts to transferring the failure from the plane of free moral decision to that of necessity. It would mean, in other words, to view the failure as inevitable. But since the church was founded by Christ Himself, to concede that it could not but fail in its mission, is to ascribe to Christ less than divine power. This the New Testament consistently precludes. Divine grace was copiously provided to carry the church through every test. With Paul the church might say, "But thanks be to God, who in Christ always leads us in triumph, and through us spreads the fragrance of the knowledge of Him everywhere."[3] As there was no compelling reason why Adam should have failed in the first place, there was no compelling necessity why the church should fail either. On the other hand, the church being composed of free moral persons was liable to failure as the result of wrong decisions. This liability to sinfulness and failure is inherent in freedom. This recognition safeguards the divine origin of the church while allowing for the historical reality of its failure.

Church historians detail the gradual departure of Christianity from apostolic faith and life. For our purpose it suffices to sketch under five headings[4] basic areas in which a shift from the primitive Christian position occurred in the church.

1. *Scission in the Body of the Church.* One of the most obvious symptoms of spiritual sickness, the growing scission in the body of the church, caused the rift between the clergy and the laity. In the earliest stage the whole church was regarded as "a chosen race, a royal priesthood, a holy nation."[5] The edifice of the church was conceived as "built upon the foundation of the apostles and prophets, Christ Jesus Himself being the chief cornerstone."[6] Individual believers were likened to "living stones" and exhorted to be built "into a spiritual house, to be a holy priesthood, to offer spiritual sacrifices acceptable to God through Jesus Christ."[7] There was no dichotomy here between clergy and laity; the church was a representative democracy in which elders and deacons exercised no greater authority than that of "shepherds of the flock."

But indifference of the laymen to their own spiritual privileges led to a gradual transfer of authority to the elected leadership or to those who by reason of charismatic endowment were better qualified to exercise a leading role in the church. Spiritual privileges entailed responsibilities which the majority tended to shrug off. Complacent human nature finds it easier to delegate the care of one's soul to another whose piety is beyond question. On the other hand, a measure of authority begets hunger for more authority. Authority unchecked tends to become absolute. A check against all-absorbing authority would have been an enlightened and resilient laity. But the dispirited citizenry of the Roman empire was no more willing to assume its share of responsibility in the religious sphere than in the political. The universal depletion of moral energy could not but affect the spiritual tone of the church in the post-apostolic age. That the church retained as much of its élan down into the days of Constantine was a perennial marvel to the pagan world, betokening the transcendent excellence of its source.

As the laity was willing to relinquish more and more of its spiritual responsibilities, the clergy assumed more than its rightful share. The original democracy of the church expressed in the concept of the "universal priesthood of believers" gave place to a clerical oligarchy domineering over an increasingly passive laity. Gnostic thought with its stress on the sufficiency of *pistis* "faith" for the common believer, while *gnosis* "knowledge" was the badge of the elect few, strengthened this trend. It was a tragic irony that heresies, even while being openly resisted, had the subtle quality of leaving a permanent imprint on the thinking of their opponents.

Whereas the original view in the church was that "there is one Mediator between God and men, the Man Christ Jesus,"[8] excluding thereby angelic or human mediation in man's confrontation with God, the view which prevailed during the Middle Ages was that laymen had no direct access to God except through the priest who admitted him into the church through baptism, held his eternal salvation in his hands by the ministration of the sacraments, and prepared him for death through extreme unction. This disparagement of the spiritual autonomy of the laymen, lost to the church the immense reservoir of moral energy latent in lay participation in the life and work of the church.[9]

In the nature of things it was foreseeable that elders or bishops of leading churches, usually in the larger cities of the empire, would gain at first administrative and later spiritual ascendancy over their peers in neighboring churches. Once started this process gained momentum until eventually the bishop (overseer) of Rome became the pope of the Western Church and the bishop of Constantinople became the patriarch of the Eastern Church. And when the two halves of the political empire went their separate ways, it was inevitable that the Western and Eastern Churches would split along the same lines, as in fact they did in 1054.

If the "sickness unto death" of the medieval church was to a large extent the result of the rift between the clergy and the laity, then the only way to spiritual rebirth was for that rift to be healed. This would mean a restoration of the laity to its proper role in the church. But what we witness during this period is an ever-growing drive on the part of the hierarchy to define and consolidate its privileges. The crystallization of the doctrine of the sacraments which reached its final form in the *Four Books of Sentences* by Peter the Lombard (1100? - 1160) served only to aggravate the rift.

2. *Conception of Salvation*. Just as damaging to the spiritual health of the church was the doctrine of salvation by works which crept

slowly into popular theology. Christians of Jewish background were particularly prone to fall into this perversion of the gospel, as the epistle to the Galatians makes poignantly clear. The gospel, far from being regarded as the good news of the remission of sins by faith in Christ, came gradually to be thought of as a new law. The very nature of Roman society, with its strong tradition of government by law, rendered the nascent church susceptible to the inroads of legalism. One consequence of this was that the doctrine of righteousness by faith, which lies at the heart of the gospel, acquired a forensic or legal tinge alien to its true intent.

Man's natural pride demands that he work out his own salvation so that he may have something to boast about. To place man's hope of salvation entirely on God's grace runs counter to deeply ingrained psychological tendencies. At the basis of every pagan scheme of salvation lie meritorious works. As a result baptism, participation in the Lord's Supper, even martyrdom, gained the status of "works." To these were added fasts, celibacy, acts of penance, pilgrimages, flagellations, building of churches, and in due time participation in the Crusades against the Saracens, Turks, or even heretics. Augustine stands almost alone among patristic writers in his insistence upon salvation by grace, although unfortunately his position carried predestinarian overtones.

In the predominant climate of salvation by works, the reason for Christ's death on the cross, which was intuitive to primitive Christianity, became a stumbling block for the medieval thinker.

One misconception led inevitably to another. Eventually the notion that some people, the saints, performed more good deeds than the "law" required gained standing in theology. These supererogatory works of Christ and the saints, it was believed, constitute a treasury of merits which the church can make available to needy sinners. From this to the notion of selling these good works through indulgences was but one step. Though indulgences were granted at first as recompense for services rendered to the church or for penance done, gradually such services were replaced by money payments, and finally by the scandalous abuses and preposterous claims denounced by Wycliffe, Luther, and other Reformers.

Another by-product of the false concept of salvation by works was

Flagellants. Self-punishment developed as one of the ways men tried to find favor with God. Latin inscription reads: "They sacrifice to Satan, and not to God." Facsimile of a miniature which appeared in Augustine's *City of God*. Historical Pictures Service, Chicago.

sacramentarianism, that is, the belief that baptism and the sacrament of the eucharist, as the Lord's Supper came to be known, had a quasi-magical effect upon the recipient guaranteeing his salvation. Independent of the character of the administrant or the faith of the recipient, the sacrament was efficacious to the purpose intended *ex opere operato*—by virtue of the action itself. With good Jewish and pagan precedent, priests must have something to offer. What more natural than to construe the Lord's Supper, once the joyful commemoration of "the Lord's death until He comes," into the perpetual sacrifice of the mass in pious disregard for the once-for-all nature of the sacrifice of Christ on the cross.

Inexorably all schemes of salvation by works only served to perpetuate human bondage. The very millstone of legalism, which Christ came to remove from the necks of men, was again bound on. As a rule, the masses who worshiped in the beautiful cathedrals of Europe never experienced the power with which Christ made men free. The Gothic cathedrals with their spires pointing to heaven, erected with the labor of love of many generations, stand as mute symbols of man's groping for a good which eluded him. Salvation as man's own achievement remains forever elusive, an illusion.

3. *The Position of the Scriptures*. There is no question that the original *kerygma,* or proclamation, of the good news was Biblically centered. The gospel writers insisted that the decisive events in the ministry of Christ happened in fulfillment of the Scriptures. Peter, in his sermon on the Day of Pentecost, authenticated his interpretation of the Christ-event by repeated appeals to the Old Testament. In this he was but following the pattern established by Christ Himself, who, on the walk to Emmaus, "beginning with Moses and all the prophets," interpreted to two of His disciples "in all the Scriptures the things concerning Himself."[10] The early church took its stand squarely upon the divine authority of the Old Testament.

As apostolic writings, or writings produced under apostolic authority, gained equal standing with those of the Old Testament, the church was believed to have been "built upon the foundation of the apostles and prophets."[11] The apostles spoke as eyewitnesses of the Lord and enjoyed in a special measure the guidance of the Spirit. Their written instructions were consequently prized as normative and regarded as of equal authority with the other Scriptures.[12] As a source book for devotional reading, and as the most valuable weapon in combating the Gnostic heresies, for all practical purposes the church had a canon of the New Testament by the end of the second century.

But whereas in the first few centuries the Scriptures enjoyed in the church the position of sole rule of faith and practice, gradually an oral tradition of which the hierarchy deemed itself the depository gained with them equal, or almost equal, footing. As a third competitor for authority came the patristic writings of the post-apostolic age to which, in the theological disputations of the Middle Ages, an uncritical appeal was made quite as often as to the Scriptures themselves.

Forced to divide their authority with tradition and the patristic literature, locked in an unknown language to the masses of Europe, unread by the illiterate majority, the Scriptures sank into practical oblivion during the Dark Ages. The church, deprived of its anchorage in the Scriptures and untutored by their eternal truths, fell prey to the theological tours de force of scholasticism. It was left to the Waldenses and Cathari, Lollards and Hussites, harbingers of the Reformation, to discover the Bible's renovating power. The Reformation restored it to its rightful position as the source of spiritual enlightenment and the test of every religious doctrine.

4. *Union of Church and State.* Having weathered victoriously the storms of imperial persecution, the church experienced its worst setback when imperial favor was thrust upon it. In identifying its future with that of a given culture or power, the church denied thereby its universality and transcendent character. Its witness henceforth was muffled by the necessity to court the favor of the powers that supported it. But the majesty of the Roman Empire was poor substitute for the majesty of Christ as the Lord of the church. Constantine's convocation of the Council of Nicea was a foreshadow of the ascendancy other emperors would claim upon the church. Reaction against this ascendancy brought about the bitter contest for supremacy between the papacy and the Holy Roman Empire which fills so many chapters of medieval history. If the principle of separation of church and state announced by Christ in the formula, "Render therefore to Caesar the things that are Caesar's, and to God the things that are God's,"[13] had been strictly adhered to, the church would have been spared these

terrible woes. Nor would the stigma of having promoted the religious wars that followed the Reformation lie upon its conscience.

After leaning for almost a century on the arm of the state, the Christian church trembled when Alaric's Visigoths sacked Rome in the year 410. The vulnerability of the secular power upon which it had relied provoked a wave of consternation that reached even Jerome in the seclusion of his monastery in Bethlehem. To many it seemed that, if the established political order should fall, the church would also fall. The crisis elicited from the pen of Augustine his *opus magnum, The City of God.* But for all his perspicacity Augustine did not alert the church against the peril of its concubinage with the state.

The church should not be made a tool of the state, as was the obvious but undeclared aim of Constantine; nor should it seek to control the state as if incapable of fulfilling its mission without political support. Asking support from the political powers, the church forfeited its claim of being a divine institution against which the powers of hell cannot prevail.[14] Dependence upon the state more than once blinded the church to its moral and spiritual responsibilities and made it conspire in attempts to stifle that freedom of conscience which is the very breath of its own life. Every effort to silence heretics by the power of the sword rather than the Spirit was tacit admission to the spiritual bankruptcy which did not fail to impress reflective minds.

5. *Loss of Sense of Mission.* A major factor contributing to the loss of the sense of mission was the development of the monastic ideal. Withdrawal from the world rather than the conversion of the world became the ideal to which thousands of Christians committed themselves. The Oriental provenance of this mystical-contemplative mood is easily recognized. It was fostered by the Neoplatonic mysticism which invaded the church after Plotinus. It had its wholesome aspects; but, carried to an extreme, it overshadowed the fact that the church, even though not of this world, had a mission to the world. Quietism and ascetic trends promoted by Gnostic dualism lured the church away from its dynamic drive. Lay passivism and clerical secularism conspired to bring about the spiritual lethargy which held the church in its deadening grip so much of the time.

In view of the changes undermining its vitality, loss of its sense of mission was inevitable. The day came when the church—which had been invested with the commission to go and "make disciples of all nations,"[15] and which in a first outburst of enthusiasm had made gigantic strides toward this goal—put a premium on flight from the world rather than the conquest of the world for Christ. After two centuries of constant expansion, during which the knowledge of Christ was blazoned from Spain in the west to Parthia in the east and from England in the north to Nubia in the south, the momentum of the church began to slacken. There were mass accretions when, under Constantine and his successors on the Byzantine throne, it became politically expedient to claim church affiliation. But these can hardly be credited to the missionary zeal of the church proper. In fact it may well be that this entrance en masse of nominal converts into the ranks of the church was a major factor in lowering its spiritual tone.

It is a sad commentary on the state of the church that in the fourth and fifth centuries missions among the pagan tribes of Europe were carried on much more vigorously by the Arians, in spite of their theological deviations, than by the champions of Nicean orthodoxy. Thus it happened that the Heruli, Ostrogoths, Vandals, Franks, and Lombards first heard the gospel from Arian missionaries. The best known among these unsung heroes was Ulfilas, who labored for the conversion of the Visigoths and whose chief monument was the translation of the Scriptures into Gothic. Evidence that the church retained greater vitality in its periphery than at its human center is the remarkable work that the Irish missionaries Columba, Columbanus, and Gallus carried out for the conversion of Scotland, northern England, and the barbarians of the Continent. Of like apostolic zeal was the Anglo-Saxon Boniface who introduced Christianity to the Bavarians and Thuringians in Germany.

While the church was making slow gains in central and northern Europe, it suffered a severe setback when the Near East and North Africa were swept by the Islamic conquests. In 711 the Saracens crossed the straits of Gibraltar into Spain and crushed the kingdom of the Visigoths. France itself was invaded, and not until 732 was the threat to Europe removed by the victory of Charles Martel over the Moors in the battle of Tours.

The church was stalled. By and large it had lost its sense of mission. Little or no concerted effort was made to reintroduce the gospel into the lands overrun by the followers of Mohammed. Except for sporadic attempts, such as that of Francis of Assisi, who preached to the Sultan of Egypt, or of Raymond Lull of Spain, who died a martyr's death in his mission to Tunis in 1315, Christian Europe remained unconcerned over the conversion of the world. The Crusades were never missionary enterprises and were only undertaken when the Seljuk Turks, who had occupied Jerusalem, forbade the visit to the holy places by Christian pilgrims. Still later a distracted Europe gazed with indifference upon the Turkish occupation of the Balkan peninsula and the fall of Constantinople. That Eastern Europe was the domain of the separated brethren of the Greek Orthodox Church partially accounts for the fact that not a finger was stirred to the rescue. Once again, even after the light of the Reformation had broken into the darkness of the Middle Ages, no systematic effort was ever made by Christianized Europe to conquer the Turks by the power of the Word rather than by the power of the sword.

NOTES AND REFERENCES

1. Acts 17:6.
2. Matthew 28:18-20.
3. 2 Corinthians 2:14.
4. The list here offered is believed to be representative, though it is by no means exhaustive. Complete unanimity in the compilation of such writs of indictment is scarcely to be expected, but it is fair to say that a greater degree of agreement might be found today than at any other time in the history of the church. Practically every one of the items discussed might be found in the agenda of the Second Vatican Council. No claim is made that the order of the items in the list is particularly significant.
5. 1 Peter 2:9.
6. Ephesians 2:20.
7. 1 Peter 2:5.
8. 1 Timothy 2:5.
9. A. Neander, *General History of the Christian Religion and Church,* Vol. 1, p. 379, makes the following apposite remark: "The clergy were not the first to derive from the unevangelical theory respecting a distinctly priestly caste the inference which lay not very remote, that the fountain of the divine word was to be approached only by themselves; that the laity must depend for all their instruction on divine things simply on the clergy, without being entitled to the original source itself," adding that the laity were likewise to be blamed for using the "distinction between a spiritual and a secular class" as a pretext to set up for themselves a "convenient Christianity" and thus excuse themselves from studying the Bible first hand.
10. Luke 24:27.
11. Ephesians 2:20.
12. See 2 Peter 3:15, 16.
13. Matthew 22:21.
14. See Matthew 16:18.
15. Matthew 28:18.

Chapter 13

The Unfinished Reformation

The failure of the church explains the delay of the long-expected advent of Christ; it is the reason the kingdoms of this world have not as yet become the kingdom of our Lord Jesus Christ. Had the church fulfilled its mission, secular history and redemptive history would, as time merged into eternity, long since have coalesced into one.

This delay now spans almost two millennia. And the believer's faith is stretched to the breaking point to admit that, notwithstanding the delay, God is still active in history, and that His redemptive plan will eventually triumph. Under the strain produced by such a delay, existentialist theologians would have us believe that time is a meaningless interlude and that only the present moment of decision is vital.[1] To Bultmann no *eschaton* is to be expected in the last day, but "every moment has eschatological possibilities" in the sense that the Christ-event may have significance for the individual at any moment of decision. According to Bultmann, the "expectation of an end of the world which is to come in time belongs to mythology."[2] In other words, to existentialist theologians the second advent of Christ is another myth that must be discarded now that humanity is come of age.

In spite of its claims, the existentialist solution does not remove the threat of meaninglessness which hangs over the head of twentieth-century men. On the contrary, it only intensifies this threat. Much more enlightening is the position of S. Mowinckel, the Scandinavian theologian, when he writes, "Christian faith, alone, can *give meaning to history,* and it insists upon doing so. The goal and meaning are given by the term 'the kingdom of God'; and the gate to this kingdom is Christ, and history's course is the way to Christ."[3]

In the same vein Rheinhold Niebuhr wrote: "Christianity embodies the whole of history in its universe of meaning because it is a religion of revelation which knows by faith of some events in history, in which the transcendent source and end of the whole panorama of history is disclosed."[4]

Christianity as a religion of revelation recognizes history as the arena of God's activity. Enlightened by the revelation contained in the Holy Scriptures, the Christian is led to believe that what is significant in history is primarily that which affects the church as the instrument of God's redemptive plan. Whatever does not affect the church or its mission is peripheral. To say that it is peripheral is not to say it is meaningless, but only to say it does not occupy the center of the stage. It has already been shown that much of the political and religious history prior to Christ acquires meaning as chapters in the preparation of the world for the reception of the gospel. This interpretation of history dates back to Eusebius of Caesarea and has roots in the New Testament's stress on "the fullness of time."[5]

Though not subscribing to any Christian view of history, R. G. Collingwood was right when he wrote: "Any history written on Christian principles will be of necessity universal, providential, apocalyptic, and periodized."[6] It could not be otherwise. It is *universal,* because God's redemptive plan embraces all of mankind. It is *providential,* since it presupposes God's active concern for the execution of His purpose which is carried out, not on some suprahistorical plane, but on the stage of this world. It is *apocalyptic,* because it looks forward to the glorious triumph of the church at Christ's second coming. And it is *periodized* in the sense that it divides all history as B.C. or A.D. on the basis of the centrality of Christ's incarnation, life, passion, death, resurrection, and ascension in the execution of God's plan of redemption. But this very event anchors Christianity in history and precludes any misconception as to its nature. When the Son of God took upon Himself human nature, He inaugurated a new era for mankind—the last. In a very real sense the *eschaton,* the last age, has begun, and it will continue until it ushers in the second advent of Christ.[7]

Of the four criteria which characterize the Christian view of history, the most relevant to the objective of this chapter is the providential. Providence is God's active concern in history, particularly the history of the church, which makes ample allowance for man's freedom. There is no denying that the church has repeatedly fallen short of its divine mission. Nevertheless the church is still the object of God's supreme regard and will continue to be until its ultimate triumph. Failure may be followed by restoration and sickness by healing.

The history of the Christian church is not altogether different from that of the Israelite community with its light and shade, victories and defeats. But the analogy breaks down at this point: The duties and privileges of the Israelite community, as a result of failure, were transferred to the Christian church, which is called the new Israel, or the "Israel of God."[8] But no such transfer of obligations and rewards is contemplated for the Christian church. It must experience renewal and renovation, to be sure, but it belongs to the last age, and its life must suffer no discontinuity. Its God-given mission carries with it the pledge of final triumph at the second advent.

If the church, which is a product of the gospel, has been in its visible and institutionalized form "shot through and through with contradictions to the gospel," to use a phrase of K. S. Latourette,[9] then the most significant events in the unfolding of history must be those which bespeak renewal and restoration of the body of Christ. Divine providence must be assumed to be active in the totality of history. Although in most areas it eludes positive identification, it should be possible to recognize its operation in those areas which particularly affect the life of the church. Reflecting upon his imprisonment in Rome, Paul was impelled to affirm in a triumph of faith, "What has happened to me has really served to advance the gospel."[10] In this one epigrammatic insight Paul sees history's critical turning points as providentially ordered. Whatever happened to the church—not necessarily its failures, but certainly its trials and triumphs, all the internal experiences of rediscovery and renewal, all the external changes in the cultural and political milieu which favored the church in the fulfillment of its mission—is viewed as so many tokens of a guiding providence. As such they acquire paradigmatic significance in the sense that through them other events are illumined.

If the subjective experiences of rediscovery and renewal are difficult to gauge unless they affect the external forms of worship and life, changes in the cultural and political climate favoring the mission of the church have left their imprints upon the pages of history and should be recognizable for what they are. Prominent among these circumstantial factors is the atmosphere of freedom. Freedom is the climate of the spiritual realm. "Where the Spirit of the Lord is, there is freedom."[11] Man matures to his full, God-given potentialities only in a climate of freedom. "If the Son makes you free, you will be free indeed."[12] The Spirit is constantly at work to enlarge the area of freedom, because not only the spiritual life of the individual but that of the church itself is conditioned by it. Deprived of freedom, man lapses into subhuman existence. "For freedom Christ has set us free."[13] That was Paul's battle cry; and wherever the pure gospel has been preached, human freedom has been enlarged. First man is delivered from the bondage of sin—and there is no worse form of bondage than this—then follows delivery from the thralldom of fear, ignorance, and superstition.

Man is never greater than when he is free from all constraint except the constraint of God's love. Christ came to set man free: free from guilt and the enslavement of sin, free from the fear of death and legalistic Pharisaism. The amazing result of such deliverance can be seen in the dynamic zeal of the apostolic church. Its members acted like giants who had been bound by the age-old chains of sin but were now freed by God's forgiving grace. In the exhilaration of their newfound freedom they set out to conquer the world for Christ. No sacrifice was too great. No intimidation could unnerve them. They were in every sense new men and women with every faculty of their being quickened by the power of a new life.

To follow the trail of freedom, then, is to follow where the Spirit is leading. Demonic powers have always made this advance toward freedom as difficult as possible, and blind man has more often than not allied himself with the powers that would perpetuate his bondage. Even the church itself, appointed as the citadel of freedom and from which freedom should permeate the whole social fabric, failed to recognize the boon of freedom and ended by denying it to both its own members and those around them. It failed when in a misguided effort for survival it allied itself with the civil power. It failed when it surrendered the liberating experience of salvation by grace and returned to the stultifying concept of salvation by works. It failed when it tried to capture the transcendental meaning of God's nature and activity in the narrow formula of dogma. Starting with a religion of the Spirit, it ended with a religion of the letter, devoid of life and power.

As the principle of causality is basic in nature, said Bernhard Erling, so the discovery of a motif is basic for an interpretation of history. Following this clue of motif research, he concludes that the ultimate meaning of history is religious, and the proper theological task is the interpretation of history. To Erling, "History rightly understood becomes *Heilsgeschichte* [the story of salvation]."[14] Taking one step farther, we propose that the enlargement of freedom is the motif that introduces meaning better than any other into the history of the church and from this radiates into secular history. Freedom first of all is spiritual, from which all other freedoms, including political, are corollaries. Let it be denied that man is a free moral person created in God's image, and the foundation of all other forms of freedom is undermined. Its denial throws the gate wide open to totalitarianism. The dignity of the individual rests upon the basis that he is a free moral being responsible to God.

Freedom never shone any brighter than during Christ's ministry on this earth. Anointed by the Spirit, He came "to proclaim release to the captives . . . , to set at liberty those who are oppressed."[15] This as prophetically announced was the program of His life. The shackles of degradation, fear, and superstition which had bound man for so long were broken open at the touch of His love. For multitudes who, prior to His coming, knew nothing except degradation of body and soul, a new age dawned. Into every breast open to its influx divine love breathed new dignity. Humble fishermen stood their ground against the unjust demands of the religious establishment of the day and won their point. There was something magnificently liberating about the Christian gospel which transformed the drab lives of thousands of obscure subjects of the empire and gave them a glorious experience worth dying for. The bell of liberty never rang any louder than when Christ declared, "If the Son makes you free, you will be free indeed."[16]

In the case of most converts, outward circumstances did not materially improve. To many, in fact, embracing the gospel meant eventual imprisonment and death. The new freedom was first of all a freedom of the spirit which gave new dignity to all mankind. Much has been written on the impact of Christianity in elevating the status of women and children.[17] Its leavening effect upon society resulted eventually in the abolition of slavery, the gladiatorial games, and other forms of human degradation. That Christianity did not accomplish more with greater dispatch is due not to any inner deficiency but to the recalcitrance of human nature and the inertia of social institutions.

From the high plane of the exhilarating freedom experienced by the believers of the apostolic and subapostolic age, the church witnessed a gradual decline which prolonged itself into the Middle Ages. Evidences of this decline were touched upon in the previous chapter. The freedom enjoyed by the majority of the believers in the early centuries of the church was gradually forfeited. The tragedy of it is that no external compulsion deprived believers of their freedom in Christ. Persecution more often than not stimulated renewal of the church's life and barred from its fellowship those who would have joined its ranks from unworthy motives. Freedom was not removed by the civil authorities; it was forfeited step by step because of plain lethargy and unwillingness to bear the burden of responsibility it entailed. Freedom merely enjoyed as a possession soon ceases to be possessed. And, like health, it is appreciated most after it is lost.

First to go was the freedom of utterance. Abuse by ecstatic preachers who spoke with misguided vigor led to curtailment of this freedom, until only "authorized" speakers were allowed in the churches. The appearances of unknown or "heretical" teachers in various congregations contributed to the trend to restrict the pulpit to persons with the proper credentials. The Montanists at the end of the second century protested against such curtailment, but in vain.[18] The gift of prophetic utterance, persistently opposed for reasons of "order," eventually became only a memory.

Another freedom lost was freedom from legalism. Paul's letter to the Galatians makes painfully clear how difficult it was for the converted Jew to extricate himself from the stranglehold of a legalistic concept of religion. The epistle to the Hebrews represents another effort to liberate Jewish converts from the attachment they felt to their ancestral faith. Not only Jewish believers, however, were prone to relapse into legalism. Reliance upon works as means of salvation is latent in the religious experience of men of all races and backgrounds. Dependence upon works carries with it dependence upon ritual and ceremonies, the importance of which grows as a living communion with God dies. The steps in the transformation of Christianity from a religion of the spirit to a religion of forms may be identified in ecclesiastical history by the ever greater value attached to the sacraments. These ceremonies expand from two recognized in the writings of the New Testament to seven in the *Sentences* of Peter the Lombard (1100? - 1160), a main source of theological instruction until the Reformation. Stemming from the same trend was the growing concern about earning merit through fasts and penances. It may indeed be postulated that anxiety about one's salvation is indissolubly bound with loss of a living faith in Christ.

Still another freedom lost was the freedom from sacerdotalism. A priestly caste dominated the religious life of Egyptians, Babylonians, Romans, and Jews. Man's dialogue with God, it was taught, had to be mediated through a priest. Christianity made actual what among the Israelites had been only an ideal, the universal priesthood of the believers.[19] Christ had opened a "new and living way" of access to God.[20] All human mediation became superfluous because through Christ, as the only Mediator, man might commune with God directly. The liberating effect of such an experience must have been electrifying. It did not mean that a teaching and preaching ministry had been done away with. But it placed the responsibility for one's religious life squarely where it belonged, upon the shoulder of every individual believer. The concept of universal priesthood meant a deliberate shift from stress on externals to a stress on religion of the heart, in the tradition of Jeremiah, who taught that the ark might go, the temple and sacrifices might cease, and yet true religion need not perish as long as man held communion with God in spirit and in truth.

Of the circumstances which conspired to deprive the church of this freedom mention was made in a previous chapter. At the heart of them were clerical assertiveness and lay apathy. Administrative and teaching responsibilities of elders and deacons turned gradually into spiritual ascendancy or overlordship. The dichotomy between laity and clergy grew with lay indifference to its spiritual privileges; and within two centuries sacerdotalism was firmly entrenched in the church and

Franciscan monks. The Franciscans and other mendicant orders formed part of a renewed protest against material greed prevailing in ecclesiastical circles. Engraving by M. Adsitto. Historical Pictures Service, Chicago.

had won, as so often in history, a victory by default. Like Esau of old, the laity sold its spiritual birthright for a mess of pottage. The consequences of this unwise surrender were not fully understood until the Reformation. It is obvious that the church could not fulfill its mission preparatory to the *parousia* until the laity reassumed its full role in the life of the church.

Once the failure of the church is recognized as a major negative event in redemptive history this side of the cross, then the Reformation of the sixteenth century at the same time acquires the significance of a major positive event. It awoke the church from its medieval lethargy and made it aware not only of the need but also of the possibility of renewal of its life. It was not the first attempt to reform the church, but it certainly was the first to succeed on a large scale.

Tokens of dissatisfaction with prevalent conditions in the church were heard all along, but in most cases they were isolated voices whose echoes died with them. Attempts to reform monasticism and to improve clerical life may be seen as early as the tenth century in the Cluny movement and continued intermittently down to the fourteenth century. Such attempts came to a head at the so-called reforming Councils of Constance and Basel, both of which ended far short of the goal.

Secular authorities more than once grew restive under oppressive ecclesiastical taxation and ecclesiastical interference in political affairs. The political ambitions of the Holy Roman Empire clashed with those of the papacy.

The Concordat of Worms of 1122 marked only a temporary compromise in the struggle over the secular versus the spiritual investiture of bishops. The appearance of the mendicant orders of Dominicans and Franciscans early in the thirteenth century was a renewed protest against the material greed prevailing within high and low ecclesiastical circles.

The warm receptivity to the teachings of the Waldenses in southern France, northern Italy, and parts of Germany and Bohemia attest to a deep-felt hunger for the bread of life which a ritualistic religion could not satisfy.

The professorial activities of John Wycliffe (1320? - 1384) in Oxford, together with his translation of the New Testament into the vernacular, anticipated the coming spiritual renovation of the church.

According to Wycliffe, the Scriptures "are the only law of the church," and the church itself "is the whole company of the elect."[21] Another harbinger of the coming Reformation was John Huss, whose preaching in the Bethlehem Chapel in Prague popularized the views of Wycliffe in Bohemia. His reformatory career was cut short by martyrdom in 1415 by decree of the Council of Constance, but his teachings affected the religious life of Bohemia for generations.

Equally symptomatic of the popular discontent with a religion that no longer satisfied the deepest aspirations of the soul was the rapid spread in Germany and Holland during the later Middle Ages of mysticism with its stress on the inward and the vital in religion. Unwholesome extreme tendencies connected with this movement do not fully discredit its positive influence, as exemplified by Tauler, Eckhart, and others, which led to the foundation of the Brethren of the Common Life. The *Imitation of Christ,* probably the work of Thomas a Kempis, witnesses even today to the abiding appeal of the simple, mystical piety inherent in the movement. It certainly recovered for the church some precious insights into the Christian faith which had been obscured by the legalistic stress on the externals of religion. These and other rivulets of spiritual renewal would, in God's own good time, issue into the mighty stream of the Reformation.[22]

The Reformation did not take place in a vacuum. Its spiritual antecedents were numerous. Christians here and there in Europe were awakening to the realization that not all was well with the church. Few at first, their number multiplied until a chorus of voices clamored for a restoration of what was authentically Biblical in the faith and life of the church. Millions heard the crescendo of demand, and those whose ears were attuned to God's Spirit responded to the summons. The rank and file of Christendom was stirred, although not equally, by the breeze of renewal and reform, but it is hardly to be expected, in the light of both the Old and the New Testaments, that a massive ecclesiastical establishment should respond unanimously to a call for reform.

As the Exodus in Israelite history, the Reformation acquired the character of a revelatory event, enabling man to know in which direction the Spirit was moving. It stood as a clear declaration that the One who founded the church is actively concerned about its ultimate triumph. Once having established the church at Pentecost, God would not leave it entirely to its own fate in deistic abandon. While allowing for human freedom, God would intervene as often as needed to rescue the church from the doldrums of self-complacency.

There is precedent for this expectation in God's dealing with His people in Old Testament times. At critical points charismatic leaders did arise to redirect the steps of a miscreant people. Such Spirit-filled men were not necessarily saints. Even Elijah, who towers like a giant in his opposition to Baal worship, was, in the apropos description of James, "a man of like nature with ourselves."[23] This fact should dispose of the objection that the Reformers displayed too much human frailty. The rudeness of Luther, or the idiosyncracies of Calvin, or the compromising bias of Melanchthon no more stamp their work as purely human than the fiery disposition of Elijah or the vacillations of Peter stamp their work as merely human. The earthiness of the human vessels does not detract from the excellency of the divine power at work in such crucial moments of salvific history.

This is not meant to suggest that the reformatory movement was not tainted in many instances by association with selfish political goals. It is indeed doubtful that one may speak of authentic reformation wherever this was imposed from above by royal decree, without a genuine popular aspiration for spiritual renewal. On the other hand it is conceivable that changes in the ecclesiastic establishment prompted by the arbitrariness of a self-willed monarch like Henry VIII of England might be overruled by Providence and become at least in part an occasion for genuine spiritual awakening. The Reformation succeeded only as far as the rank and file of the church was prepared to advance. That it ended in compromise across the board is generally admitted. Its results were far from final. What no one would deny is that the Reformation set in motion a tidal wave of renewal in the life of the church, the full force of which has not as yet been spent.

There are those who see in the Reformation of the sixteenth century a mere by-product of the current of nationalism and humanism then sweeping over Europe. In the fire of the Hundred Years' War, France and England had occasion to weld together the fragments of a feudal society into integrated nations. The emerging nations proved less tractable to the papacy with its ever-shifting political interests, and they resented the drain on the national wealth by the cupidity of a secularized ecclesiastical establishment. But nationalism, whatever the forces that were propelling it forward, was but a handmaid of Providence to deliver the church from the suffocating grip of ecclesiastical opulency. In reference to the church one might say, paraphrasing the common dictum, wealth corrupts and much wealth always. A pope is reported to have remarked to Thomas Aquinas on a visit to Rome, "No longer can we say, 'Silver and gold have I none.'" Replied the astute theologian, "But neither can you say with Peter, 'In the name of Jesus Christ of Nazareth, rise up and walk.'" Apocryphal or not, this anecdote well portrays the condition of a church rich in material resources but spiritually impoverished. Nationalism, furthering its own objectives which often clashed with those of a secularized clergy, compelled the church to reassess its life and goals.

The same may be said of humanism with its stress on man and his temporal existence. It reversed the devaluation of secular life which warped medieval thought for so long. The church, under the influence of Gnostic dualism, had transferred to a heavenly sphere all bliss which man might ever hope to enjoy and thereby dissociated itself from any responsibility to make man's life on earth not merely bearable but a joyful, liberating experience. It gilded those passages in the New Testament which have an ascetic flavor and underrated those which speak of the more abundant life accessible to the believer even now. "I came," said Jesus, "that they may have life, and have it abundantly."[24]

As a divine gift, earthly existence has a value of its own. Otherworldliness is not of the essence of Christianity. Humanism recaptured this truth and created the climate for a reassessment of the dignity of marriage, family life, education, and labor. That humanism led *pari passu* to the progressive secularization of modern life may be the result of one of those unhappy reactions against the extreme medieval ascetic ideal. As Erich Kahler puts it: "Deprived of its spiritual sanction, earthly life followed its independent and unholy course."[25] And the same writer places the blame for secularization at the door of Augustine and his *De Civitate Dei* with its unwholesome dichotomy between the life of the body and the life of the spirit. On the other hand, a church still tightly bound in the swaddling clothes of medieval prudery would be even less able to entertain dialogue with modern man in a secular culture.

Another service rendered by humanism to the church was its unbounded curiosity in man's past, which lent a new impetus to classical studies and to the desire to read the Bible in the original languages. The Greek New Testament published by Erasmus in 1516, anticipating by a few years the Complutensian Polyglot edited by Cardinal Jiménez, brought forth a new era in Biblical studies and paved the way for the work of the Reformation which advanced hand in hand with the translation of the Scriptures into the vernacular languages of Europe. It has been truly said that Martin Luther did more for the Reformation with his translation of the Bible into German than in any other way. The Reformation would have stopped short in its tracks were it not for the perennial appeal of the Biblical message to men of all languages. The back-to-the-Bible slogan had not lost its timeliness but proved contemporaneous with the ever-living Christ shining from its pages.

From a Biblical view of history, then, even nationalism and humanism appear as preparatory movements for the Reformation, whatever their secular overtones. This does not mean that either one brought unmitigated blessings to the church. Indeed not. The reformed churches of northern Europe, almost without exception, became dependent on the secular powers and thus lost much of their autonomy and vitality. Although this dependence might have served a useful temporary purpose in a European transition, it does not follow that interim arrangements should be taken as normative. All that is claimed here is that the Reformation, not the ancillary movements, occupied the center of the stage in the divine scheme of things. The Reformation rode indeed on the crest of the nationalistic and humanistic waves of the late Middle Ages. For all of that the rider and not the waves claims primary attention.

That the Reformation has not been recognized for what it was, an event of the first magnitude not only in church history but in secular history as well, may account for the loss of sense of meaning in the twentieth-century appraisals of man's past. Collingwood, for example, in his preliminary survey of significant turning points in history, refers to the Renaissance but not to the Reformation.[26] The same is true of

Erich Kahler who, in his challenging book, *The Meaning of History*, dismisses the significance of the Reformation with this wry remark: "Undermined by scholastic analysis, as well as by mystical heresies which went over into the successive reform movements, the degenerated church split; its true catholicity ended and it shrank to a party, theological and political."[27]

Any attempt to find meaning in history while dismissing the most significant spiritual event of the sixteenth century as irrelevant is bound to become a pedantic chase after the insignificant.

Existential theologians have, of course, taken the easy way out by positing all of history as irrelevant and all historical interpretation as following the wisp of the whim. Reviewing the age-long search for meaning, R. Bultmann states that "the question of meaning in history was raised and answered for the first time within an outlook which believed it knew the end of history. This occurred in the Jewish-Christian understanding of history which was dependent on eschatology."[28]

But then he goes on to say that today no one may claim to know the end and the goal of history, and, therefore, the question of meaning in history is pointless. If revelation is thus discarded and secular history dissociated from divine concern, then any attempt to find meaning in history is indeed hopeless. But, as Claude Welch puts it: "The eschatology of the NT [New Testament] cannot be made into a simply vertical eschatology, with the coming of the kingdom being only the immediate relation of each moment to a transcendent realm" in the manner of Bultmann and existential theologians. "The kingdom is not only 'looked up to,' it is looked 'forward to.' The reference to the future cannot be excluded."[29] In other words, eschatology cannot be dissociated from history as a sequence of events in time. The Gnostic concept of timelessness, so prominent in Bultmann, cannot be squared with the Biblical view of redemptive history as a series of divine transactions occurring in time.[30]

Once the Reformation is seen as a paradigmatic event in redemptive history—in the sense conferred on "paradigmatic" by Eric Voegelin,[31] that is, as descriptive of revelatory events with the help of which other events acquire meaning—then all of history is bathed in new light. History is seen again as moving toward a new goal, the goal of total renewal of the church, which will usher in the advent of Christ. Of this renewal, the Reformation of the sixteenth century marked a major step. Not the final step, but one that revealed as no other the work of the Spirit in the life of the church.

And if God's Spirit was effective in the mighty works of the Reformation era, there is no reason to suppose that the church has been left stranded on the shoals of an unfinished task ever since. On the contrary, the effective agency of the Spirit must be recognized in the Puritans' struggle for freedom of worship which led to the colonization of New England in the seventeenth century, in the Pietistic and Wesleyan revivals which in the following century shook the churches in Germany and England out of their spiritual lethargy, and most certainly in the missionary movement inaugurated by William Carey which placed forcibly before the church the urgency of making Christ known to the world. As result of the missionary expansion carried by a countless host of Spirit-filled soldiers of the cross, the church for the first time in its history became truly universal.

NOTES AND REFERENCES

1. See Shirley J. Case, *The Christian Philosophy of Religion,* pages 94-100, criticizing Kierkegaard and the theology of crisis.
2. R. Bultmann, *Jesus and the World,* page 56.
3. S. Mowinckel, *The Old Testament as Word of God,* tr., page 49.
4. R. Niebuhr, *Faith and History,* page 22.
5. On the significance of "the fullness of time" see John Alzog, *History of the Church,* tr., Vol. 1, pp. 127 ff.
6. R. G. Collingwood, *The Idea of History,* page 49.
7. See 1 John 2:18.
8. Galatians 6:16.
9. K. S. Latourette, *A History of Christianity,* page 262.
10. Philippians 1:12.
11. 2 Corinthians 3:17.
12. John 8:36.
13. Galatians 5:1.
14. Bernhard Erling, *Nature and History,* page 239.
15. Luke 4:18.
16. John 8:36.
17. See Paul Wendland, *Die Hellenisch-Römische Kultur,* pages 45-47.
18. See W. A. Gifford, *The Story of Faith,* page 150.
19. See 1 Peter 2:9; Exodus 19:6.
20. Hebrews 10:20.
21. W. Walker, *A History of the Christian Church,* page 269.
22. In this connection see J. Dillenberger and C. Welch, *Protestant Christianity,* pages 4-10.
23. James 5:17.

24. John 10:10.
25. Erich Kahler, *The Meaning of History,* page 184.
26. See R. G. Collingwood, *op. cit.,* p. 57.
27. Erich Kahler, *op. cit.,* p. 132.
28. R. Bultmann, *Presence of Eternity,* page 120.
29. Claude Welch, *The Reality of the Church,* page 140.
30. For a criticism of the Gnostic-existentialist view of salvation see O. Cullman, *Christ and Time,* pages 51 ff.
31. See Erich Voegelin, *Order and History,* Vol. 1, p. 121.

Chapter 14

History as the Story of Freedom

Reviewing the historical trend in Europe from the Reformation to the French Revolution, it is almost impossible to ignore a progressive unfurling of the banner of freedom. The Reformation of the sixteenth century with its stress upon the dignity of man sounded the clarion call for the eventual enfranchisement of the common man shackled so long by the bonds of feudalism and religious absolutism.

The march toward the goal of greater religious and political freedom for the greatest number, since the ruling classes would not easily relinquish traditional privileges, was beset with obstructions at every step. It was marked by compromises adopted in 1555 to bring to a halt religious strife in Germany with the formula, *cujus regio, ejus religio* ("whose region, his religion"), *i.e.*, whoever governs the country determines the religion of the subjects. It suffered setbacks as when the Edict of Nantes was revoked by Louis XIV in 1685, forcing thousands of French Protestants into exile. The march toward freedom experienced such reverses as the repression of Puritanism in England or Jansenism in France, but it could not be permanently arrested.

Fanned by the writings of liberal authors, the winds of freedom gained momentum throughout the Age of Enlightenment until they swept Europe with hurricane force in the French Revolution and the excesses of the Napoleonic Wars. In vain would the Congress of Vienna try in 1815 to halt the irreversible trend toward a democratization of national institutions. History was on the side of freedom, and the *ancien régime* was doomed. Having once tasted the blessings of liberty, men everywhere were determined not to accept again the shackles of religious and political absolutism.

If God's effective presence in the history of the church is made manifest by recurring experiences of spiritual renewal, enabling it to fulfill its mission of mediating God's grace to the world, by the same token God's effective presence in secular history is best recognized in every movement that promotes human freedom and dignity. In this sense history is indeed the story of freedom.

But it is sheer poetic license to affirm with Benedetto Croce that "liberty is the eternal creator of history."[1] Liberty becomes a creative force only when incarnated in some individual or group. Only then the abstract ideal becomes a burning passion capable of moving mountains. But the very fact that the ideal of freedom can inspire men to the most heroic deeds shows that it belongs to the very essence of man as a son of God. Man was made for freedom. "For freedom Christ has set us free."[2] Only in a climate of freedom is man truly human. Man's dignity is inextricably and vitally related to his freedom.

Why should this be so? No materialistic philosophy can account for it. In fact, this unswerving and universal aspiration for freedom is baffling to materialistic dialecticians. Only Christianity is in position to give a satisfactory answer. According to the Scriptures, freedom is one aspect of the *imago Dei* in man. The counterpart of freedom is responsibility. Both are integral to man's dignity as a son of God. Man was created a responsible being, and his responsibility can only be meaningful in an atmosphere of freedom. Man must ever be free to respond with a Yes or a No to God's word addressed to him.

The historical trend toward greater freedom for the plodding masses has been wrongly interpreted as signifying that man's redemption is effected by the historical process. It has been suggested that, given enough time, history will almost automatically bring about man's emancipation from all forms of tyranny. This is tantamount to making history man's savior. But the Christian view of redemption is broader than emancipation from political thralldom; it involves reconciliation. Man is a rebel in chains which cannot be broken, because they are forged with the refractory links of alienation from God. Only through reconciliation with his Creator are man's Promethean bonds effectively and permanently broken. History may, at best, create the environment in which this reconciliation takes place. It does so by surrounding man with a climate of freedom in which moral decisions are possible.

Proclaiming the revocation of the Edict of Nantes, October 22, 1685. Religious and political freedom suffered a setback in France when Louis XIV revoked the edict which had granted religious toleration. Engraving by A. De Neuville. Historical Pictures Service, Chicago.

If reconciliation with God is the ultimate goal, then, although they are never the same, the historical process and redeeming grace converge toward the same end. Through the historical process Providence creates those circumstances which enhance moral and religious freedom. But moral responsibility only leads to redemption in the Christian sense if it issues into reconciliation with God through Christ. This demands a personal decision in response to divine grace.

History remains tragic because man's alienation from God cannot be overcome arbitrarily. Reconciliation cannot be achieved except through man's free response to divine love. Though tragic, history, even secular history, partakes of a redemptive design, both by revealing God's love and by creating a modicum of freedom. It takes a peculiar measure of faith to believe with Leibnitz that this is the best of all possible worlds, but once allowance is made for the brute fact of sin and rebellion, the stumbling block is removed. History is neither meaningless nor inconsequential. Scripturally it can be regarded as no other than the arena of God's activity. Even though the divine presence is shrouded in mystery, enough glimpses of God's concern have been vouchsafed to man to make the Biblical view credible. Of these intimations of a divine power that makes for righteousness, none is comparable to the insight into God's redemptive plan afforded by the cross. Anchored in history, the Christ-event makes all history reveal a providential design.

The tragedies of history, the result of man's titanic struggle for self-assertion against the threat of oblivion, should not blind us to the evidence of an overruling providence. This is nowhere clearer than in the mission of the church as the herald of the word of reconciliation through which the divine call is ever renewed to man. Through the church heaven touches earth. But the church itself would be hampered in its mission in the absence of that measure of freedom without which basic Christian decision is impossible. In the words of G. Heard, the social structure should create "those conditions of freedom wherein the maximum of creative choice is presented."[3] Every instance of progress toward greater freedom becomes, then, evidence of a divine intent to bring about the best climate for genuine Christian decision. All those social or political changes which favor genuine freedom also favor the mission of the church. From this viewpoint one should be able to discern that, in the play and counterplay of political forces, the cause of freedom stood to gain in spite of temporary setbacks, and that consciously or not mankind was ever striving for that greater freedom which makes men truly human.

To Herder "the purpose of history is the attainment of humanity, *i.e.*, (presumably) the attainment of a state of affairs where men are most truly themselves."[4] Herder's view is not inconsistent with the Biblical view, since full humanity can coexist only with true freedom. But Herder errs in making history a self-operating process. According to Paul's explanation to the Ephesians, one of the goals of redemption is that man should attain "to mature manhood, to the measure of the stature of the fullness of Christ."[5] Of itself, history cannot restore God's image in man, thus effecting the goal of history and redemption. All it can do is to provide a climate of freedom congenial with the demand for moral decision. But precisely because it can do this, it shares in the redemptive program.

The Reformation of the sixteenth century acted as a catalyst in initiating or accelerating processes which eventuated in the breakthroughs of the American and French Revolutions. By recapturing the apostolic principle of the universal priesthood of the believers, and by insisting, as Luther did, on the freedom of the Christian man, it promoted a progressive democratization of the ecclesiastical establishment. The laity, so long relegated to a dependent role in the church, was made conscious of its responsibility. Except for the participation of the laity in the cup and bread at the Communion table and congregational singing as part of divine worship, no drastic changes were immediately seen in the Lutheran and Reformed churches.

But a corollary of the principle of the universal priesthood of believers had a more immediate repercussion: the recognition of the right to private examination and interpretation of the Scriptures. This right was implied when the Scriptures were translated into the current languages of Europe and their reading encouraged as a devotional aid. This encouragement might have been nothing more than a pious counsel were it not for the fact that the newly perfected art of printing made the Word of God increasingly accessible to the millions of Europe. From the first, the press was put at the service of a Bible-oriented Reformation. Significantly, the first book printed by Gutenberg was the Vulgate Bible. A veritable flood of popular editions of the Bible in the vernacular followed in the wake of the Reformation, retaining its momentum even today.

The impact of such massive dissemination of the Scriptures has not been fully appreciated by historians. It was from the ranks of Bible readers that religious dissenters on the Continent and in England gathered most of their followers. Acquaintance with the primary source of revealed truth kept thousands from the spiritual torpor into which the reformed churches relapsed after the energies and inspiration of the Reformation had dissipated.

As the heat of theological controversies forced the Reformers to give a rational formulation to their beliefs, the danger was ever present that a hollow conformity to a creed might be substituted for a living faith grounded on a personal experience of salvation. Protestantism was not immune to a barren and cold scholasticism; in fact, it partially succumbed to it in the following centuries. What rescued it from total spiritual apathy were the dissenters and nonconformists who acted as gadflies to the established churches. An institutionalized church is ever prone to a cold formalism and heartless orthodoxy, but divine truth ever transcends the narrow bonds of a formal creed. If truth is eternally the same, man's apprehension of it is of necessity partial and progressive. Of this verity dissenters were a constant and salutary reminder. Each of them, at the risk of being branded a fanatic, stressed some aspect of revelation which others had failed to grasp. Thus Puritans and Quakers, Baptists and Presbyterians, Pietists and Methodists each made a particular contribution to a deeper understanding of the "truth as it is in Christ." John Robinson, in his farewell address to the Pilgrim Fathers, expressed the true ethos of the Reformation with crystal clearness when he bewailed the reluctance of the reformed churches to advance beyond the point where Luther or Calvin had left them and recalled their covenant with God and with one another "to receive whatsoever light or truth shall be made known to us from His Written Word."[6]

The recognition of the relative merit of different perceptions of Biblical truth, which no amount of external coercion can reduce to a generally agreed common denominator, must perforce generate a climate of irenic tolerance. But freedom of worship, which today, with exceptions, is recognized as an inalienable right, was only achieved after agonizing suffering through centuries of religious wars and persecutions.

It is easy for the secular historian to dismiss the Thirty Years' War (1618 - 1648) as the last great conflagration in Europe caused by religious rivalries. It is true that religious persecutions still occurred in France in the aftermath of the revocation of the Edict of Nantes (1685) and that the Inquisition still flared occasionally in Spain and its colonies. But for practical purposes large-scale tyranny in religion had ceased.

What is not so commonly recognized is that the breakdown of religious tyranny was the harbinger of the eventual breakdown of political tyranny which ushered in the constitutional governments of the nineteenth century. Political enfranchisement came as result either of the progressive extension of the principle of religious freedom, as in England and in the United States, or as reaction against religious absolutism, as in France. By uprooting religious dissent, whether within the established church, as in the case of the Jansenists, or outside the church, as in the case of the Huguenots, France drove the intellectuals into an anticlerical and antiroyal camp. The absolutism of the Bourbons and of a church dominated by Jesuit influence was questioned by the intelligentsia which read avidly the new books on the theory of government written by Hobbes or Locke, Montesquieu or Rousseau.

Basic to all formulations of political theory in the eighteenth century was the principle that all men were created equal and free and that the ultimate source of the political power resided with the people. Such concepts would not have gained the prestige of self-evident truth were it not for the groundwork laid by the Reformation with its insistence on the universal priesthood of the believers, and its corollary, the right of private interpretation of the Scriptures. People accustomed to question religious tradition and to test it by the norm of the Scriptures would eventually question the tradition of political absolutism as well. That some of the most vocal critics of the political status quo were taking for self-evident truths principles which derive their validity from the Scriptures, shows how pervasive the teachings of the Reformation were in the thought of the Enlightenment. Remove their Christian substratum, and these truths cease to be self-evident. The conscious effort to deny the intellectual debt of democracy to Christianity has led in our own day to new forms of absolutism incongruent with human freedom and dignity.

Let it be granted that the extension of the areas of freedom has not always enhanced the mission of the church. Emancipation from religious tyranny has often led to total break with Christianity, as if Christianity were inimical to man's highest good. The trend since the Reformation has been toward a total secularization of life and culture in all its aspects. Rebounding from medieval otherworldliness, multitudes have opted for the opposite extreme, hedonism. The principle of private interpretation of the Scriptures has often promoted rationalism at the expense of faith. And yet the fact that good has been perverted does not make the original less than good. Freedom confronts man with moral risks. Yet without freedom man would be less than human. As the arena of moral decisions, history must ever surround man with a measure of freedom. Since these moral decisions have spiritual implications of more than temporal interest, history can never be indifferent to God as the guarantor of the moral order. Through His providence God acts toward preserving and expanding the areas of freedom. To reverse this trend would be to defeat His redemptive purpose for man whose response to the divine call must ever be a response in freedom.

The history of sin is the story of the perversion of freedom. Unquestionably man has mismanaged his freedom through wrong choices. This is the Biblical account of the origin and perpetuation of sin. It will not do to say that moral decisions are transacted in the forum of one's conscience independently of external circumstances. This might be true if man were pure spirit. But he is a biosocial entity. His freedom is conditioned by his physical and social environment. In addition, he is conditioned by his historical position in time. Whether conscious of it or not, man is a historic entity as well, subject to all the biases and prejudices of his age. What must be redeemed is not man in abstract, but man who bears the mark of historical conditioning upon every fiber of his being and every strand of his thought. If man is to remain a responsible moral agent capable of religious decisions, evidently he must not be allowed to be crushed by the weight of his historical past. Providence sees to it that a modicum of freedom is preserved for man by the creation of safeguards which assume the form of what B. Croce called "institutions of liberty."

Examples of such institutions are constitutional guarantees and bills of rights, the need for which was increasingly felt as man experienced the crushing weight of the pyramiding political edifice. Characteristically enough, popular sentiment forced the framers of the American Constitution to include a clause safeguarding freedom of religion, the first in the Bill of Rights. In France, after the hectic days of the Reign of Terror, Camille Jordan passed through the National Assembly in 1797 a bill declaring full freedom of religion for both Catholics and Protestants. Similar safeguards were later incorporated in the constitutions of most nations of Europe and America, even though remaining a dead letter in some instances until enlightened conscience demanded enforcement.

It follows that secular history, though often hostile to the church, is never allowed to carry its hostility to the point of totally defeating the redemptive mission of the church. As freedom is both the goal and the prerequisite of redemption, then the church, if it is going to fulfill its mission at all, must enjoy a measure of freedom to the very end.

Redemption, in the Biblical sense, is God's activity directed toward reconciling man to Himself. This activity is carried out in the historical plane through the church in whose bosom Christ was born and whose presence with the church makes her redemptive work an extension of the incarnation. It is conceivable that God might have chosen to save man without the agency of the church, without the "foolishness of preaching,"[7] without making the gift of faith dependent on the spoken word. But the plain Scriptural fact is that as God chose Israel of old as the bearer of light to the Gentiles, so He chose the New Testament church as the agency to make known to the world His redemptive purpose.

But since Christ chose to send His disciples to the world as ambassadors of reconciliation, as He Himself had been sent into the world,[8] then redemptive history, which climaxed in the cross, becomes coextensive with the history of the church as bearer of the good news. Redemptive history ceases to be merely a record of transactions enacted in the distant past. It is that, but the last page cannot be written until the church fulfills its mission and the second coming of Christ is seen.

In consequence, secular history derives its meaning by providing the backstage to redemptive history. It is the story of man's response in love or hostility to the message proclaimed through the church. At the same time it is the story of man's rival attempts at working out his own salvation independently of God's proffered grace. And the futility of such attempts fills the annals of man's tragic past.

REFERENCES

1. Benedetto Croce, *History as the Story of Liberty.*
2. Galatians 5:1.
3. G. Heard, quoted in M. C. D'Arcy, *The Meaning and Matter of History,* page 293.
4. W. H. Walsh, *An Introduction to the Philosophy of History,* page 135.
5. Ephesians 4:13.
6. Edward Winston, *Brief Narration,* quoted in Alexander Young, *Chronicles of the Pilgrim Fathers,* page 397.
7. 1 Corinthians 1:21, KJV.
See John 17:18.

Chapter 15

Mankind's Finest Hour

Man's most conspicuous achievement of the last two hundred years, the scientific revolution, has transformed the face of the earth and quickened the pace of life. As a result of successive breakthroughs in science and technology, the possibility of a life of affluence and leisure has come for the first time to the reach of millions in our modern world.

It would be idle to recount these scientific achievements to a public that has become accustomed to take progress and change in its stride. Such spectacular feats as the harnessing of atomic energy for peaceful purposes, the ever-wider use of electronic computers to do man's chores, wholesale automation, the rocketing of astronauts to the moon, scarcely thrill sophisticated man in the second half of the twentieth century. That universities are opening computerized information-and-retrieval systems to their students enabling them to obtain maximum information on a subject by simply operating dials, barely makes news nowadays. Ocean water is being desalinized for irrigation in plants progressively more efficient, opening the possibility of cultivating vast new tracts of desert land. In some quarters, indeed, it is taken for granted that science may solve any problem that may be intelligently proposed.

In this bright picture of scientific escalation there are, nevertheless, some perplexing shades. While some nations move rapidly forward as the result of technological know-how, the economic gap between developed and underdeveloped nations increases. The tension thus created is ominous. The population explosion which threatens to catapult the population of the world into the six-billion bracket within thirty years is bound to wipe out any progress made toward feeding the multitudes of earth. Even with the most favored

Giant Saturn-V rocket blasts astronauts into earth orbit. Twentieth-century man has become accustomed to rapid technological progress. United Press International Photograph.

nations helping the less favored ones, mankind faces total disaster.

Furthermore, if this veritable explosion of scientific knowledge which is the glory of our age provokes nothing but a wave of insatiable material ambitions, it will prove in the end to be mankind's greatest delusion. If the more abundant life promised by the advance of technology should lead to nothing better than a harvest of gross materialism, man will once more have sold his spiritual heritage for a mess of pottage. If man, liberated from degrading poverty by the miracles of science, does not use his newfound freedom to perfect his spiritual life and rediscover God, his lot will be no better than that of Faust in Goethe's tragedy, who, in exchange for the world and its glory, sold his soul to the devil.

Material progress is a blessing if it is the preparatory stage for spiritual and moral advance on the same magnificent scale. Its function in the divine program may be identical to the miracles performed by Christ in His earthly ministry. In healing the leper, or restoring sight to the blind, or feeding the multitudes, the divine Physician had in mind a higher goal. The miracle, never an end in itself, was only a means to further spiritual restoration. If the leper whose body had been cleansed did not aspire to the cleansing of his soul, the miracle would have been in vain. If the man born blind, having seen the light of the sun, did not recognize in Christ the Sun of Righteousness, it would have been better for him to remain in darkness. If the multitudes, having had their material hunger miraculously satisfied on the loaves and fishes, did not desire the Bread of Life to satisfy their spiritual vacuity, they were not better off, but infinitely worse.

If the explosion of growing aspirations which propels nations and individuals to harness nature and place its unlimited resources at the service of human welfare—if this explosion, I repeat, will not generate at the same time the desire to reach greater heights in the life of the spirit, man will have lost his finest opportunity. The consequences of such a blunder stagger the imagination. If the most promising cultural achievements are not destined to evaporate in the holocaust of a nuclear war, the unprecedented mobilization of technical and scientific skills must be matched by a similar mobilization of the moral forces of humanity. To the technical know-how which has benefited man materially there must correspond a faith that will lift him spiritually. Science which frees man from misery and obscurantism must have reinforcement by a religion that liberates man from the threat of meaninglessness and spiritual death.

In spite of all warnings, tragedy is taking shape before our eyes. The economic emancipation of mankind is not paralleled by a similar spiritual emancipation. The progressive victory over poverty and disease is not followed by a comparable victory over spiritual apathy and moral turpitude. The pages of history abound with examples of nations who won wars but lost peace. The Athenians, victorious over the Persians at Marathon and Plataea, succumbed two generations later to their inability to break through the narrowness of their political views. There is nothing more hideous and tragic for twentieth-century man than to win the war against poverty and social inequities and lose the fight against depravity and sin.

To mankind today is offered the best opportunity of its history for a spiritual advance without precedent. The age-old thralldom of ignorance, poverty, and sickness is being shattered all down the line. One might say without exaggeration that Providence is doing for mankind today, through the agency of science, miracles as great as those with which God favored Judea and Galilee through the ministry of Christ. The means are different, but the source and the objectives are the same. Modern scientific wonders, as well as the wonders recorded in the Gospels, were meant to be opportunities for the even greater miracle of man's spiritual redemption. In multiplying bread or healing the sick, Jesus was but predisposing the human heart to receive the greater gift of salvation. However, without the effective response of grateful hearts, Christ can no more complete His work of grace today than He could help those nine lepers who did not return to express their gratitude.

Automation is the order of the day. Factories are being geared for faster production. Banks, insurance companies, and even the Government employ the services of electronic computers to expedite services. Automatic pilots guide planes and keep them on course, while others yet more sophisticated guide moon-bound rockets with uncanny precision. Automation is another gift of science which promises to revolutionize modern life. There is nothing automatic, though, in the realm of the spirit. Without the effective cooperation of the individual will, no miracle takes place, no victory over self is won, no spiritual progress is made. Material well-being engendered through science creates the necessary conditions for spiritual emancipation, but this takes place only when divine grace meets the response of faith.

Man cooperates with divine providence by using the resources of science to push back the specter of famine and to overcome the ravages of disease. Every program of economic and social assistance does its part in removing the blinders which keep man from recognizing his opportunities for spiritual growth. Every effort made to eradicate degrading poverty and stultifying ignorance contributes to the advancement of the kingdom of heaven, because it creates more favorable conditions for the seed of the gospel to germinate and produce fruit.

History is the arena of God's activity and will remain so until the goal of history is achieved with the bringing to perfection and fulfillment of all things in Christ, both "things in heaven and things on earth."[2] This view alone does justice to the facts of history and the statements of the Scriptures. The scientific accomplishments of the present age are man's accomplishments, and yet these achievements have been providentially guided. They fulfill a purpose in the divine plan. As such they are eternally significant and render the present age meaningful in the unfolding drama of redemption.

But what has been said above does not exhaust the full significance to be attached to present-day technological advances which for some revolutionize every aspect of life. One obvious result of such advances has been to reduce our divided and fragmented planet to one world. Ever more rapid methods of transportation have shrunk distances to the vanishing point. Stationary-orbit satellites momentarily retransmit news to almost any point on the globe. Whether the prospect is pleasant or not, all nations are becoming next-door neighbors. The globe may be circumnavigated in less than twenty-four hours by jet or ninety minutes by a rocket. More and more statesmen are forced to think in global terms. What affects any point of the earth has increasing repercussions on other points.

If the prospect of preaching the gospel to all the world might seem utopian to previous generations, the task is becoming more and more feasible as technological progress is put to the service of printing and preaching the gospel. It might well be that science, which was in a very deep sense promoted by the Reformation, was meant to render this very service to the cause of Christ.

As a result of the increase of knowledge in all areas, a more accurate understanding of the Bible than ever before is possible today. Better and more rapid facilities for printing and distributing the sacred page are being used. The science of linguistics has rendered the translation of the Bible into the languages of the world a more reliable enterprise. Radio and television know no boundaries, and the ubiquitous transistor radio puts countless millions within the reach of the gospel preacher. As problems resulting from the population explosion and arbitrary restrictions on travel and exchange of information have multiplied, so have the means to overcome these barriers. Radio waves can penetrate where no evangelist can freely preach.

The Bible speaks of a climactic end to human history. It is well-nigh impossible to read its pages and not be impressed with the fact that this age is the last. Human history, as we know it, will not endure beyond the day when God's redemptive plan is fulfilled. One harbinger of the approaching climax is that "this gospel of the kingdom" is to be preached in all the world as a witness to all nations.[3] This statement of Christ, which challenged the faith of previous generations of believers, is meeting a glorious fulfillment under our very eyes.

Through the enlargement of the areas of freedom, as well as by the well-timed advances of science, divine providence has been leading history to its appointed goal. In the breathtaking tempo in which world-shaking events succeed one another, those who take the Scriptures seriously will recognize history's last hour. Once more eternity will invade time and swallow it up in victory. To Christ's declaration, " 'Surely I am coming soon,' " the church fervently responds, "Amen. Come, Lord Jesus!"[4]

REFERENCES

1. Matthew 4:4.
2. Ephesians 1:10.
3. Matthew 24:14.
4. Revelation 22:20.